logolounge 3

2,000 International Identities by Leading Designers

GLOUCESTER MASSACHUSETTS

ROCKPORT PUBLISHERS

Bill Gardner and Catharine Fishel

First published in the United States of America by
Rockport Publishers, a member of
Quayside Publishing Group
33 Commercial Street
Gloucester, Massachusetts 01930-5089
Telephone: (978) 282-9590
Fax: (978) 283-2742
www.rockpub.com

Library of Congress Cataloging-in-Publication Data

Gardner, Bill.
    LogoLounge 3 : 2,000 international identities by leading designers /
Bill Gardner and Catharine Fishel.
        p.   cm.
    Includes index.
    ISBN 1-59253-238-1 (hardcover)
    1. Logography—Design Catalogs. 2. Corporate image—Catalogs.
3. Designers—Directories. I. Title: LogoLounge Three. II. Title: 2,000 international identities by leading designers. III. Fishel, Catharine M. IV. Title.

ISBN-13: 978-1-59253-238-4
ISBN-10: 1-59253-238-1

10 9 8 7 6 5 4 3 2 1

Design: Gardner Design
Layout & Production: *tabula rasa* graphic design
Production Coordinator: Elisabeth Owens/Gardner Design
Cover Image: Gardner Design

Printed in China

To Cathy, Brian, Troy, and Gail, my partners and co-navigators in LogoLounge; to Susan, Luke, and Mason of Gardner Design, for keeping the ship leveled out when I bury myself in these books; thanks especially to Elisabeth of Gardner Design for her tireless diligence in assembling the work of our exceptional members for publication; to Kristin at Rockport for keeping these books a joy to produce; and mostly to Andrea and Molly, the loves of my life.

–Bill Gardner

To Alex, Andrew, and Sam, my sons and mentors—thank you.

–Catharine Fishel

contents

introduction

LogoLounge.com and the LogoLounge book series have been so overwhelmingly embraced by the design community that at times I almost feel a bit embarrassed. Members of the site and readers of the books have asked time and again about their success. The marriage of the site and its books are complex when you start to consider all they offer and the diverse ways they are used. But I have narrowed the answer down to one word: context.

There's another word that is nearly as critical as context—its near twin, content. Since the site's inception at the end of 2001, LogoLounge.com members have submitted more than 37,000 logos as of early 2006. Our thousands of members represent every top-tier identity firm in the world and nearly every nation on Earth. They also represent the genius of small studios that know how to help their clients thrive as top-tier competitors.

Every day, more logos are uploaded to LogoLounge.com, and as amazing and stimulating as these thousands of logos are, they would be perilously close to useless without context. Imagine your desk heaped with 37,000 individual logos, each on a separate slip of paper and in no particular order. It would be of modest value to anyone. Looking for logos of globes, or birds, or leaves, or for a coffee house, or the letter "E"? You could just start digging and, depending on your stamina, you might eventually find something inspirational. Or, if you really had months to invest, you could start to organize the heap.

This absurd situation is pretty close to what happens when you try to find something specific in the mass of books on your shelves, each with its contents randomly organized. Spontaneity is good, but not when you're under the gun and need very specific reference. This is why the book you're holding is filled with 2,000 logos, meticulously organized to allow you to intuitively find inspiration wherever you look and exactly where you expect it.

To add to the book's value, its 2,000 logos are further organized on a companion website at www.logolounge.com/book3. When you log onto this site, you will be able to use the same search tools that LogoLounge.com members use when searching the nearly 38,000 logos on the site. You can search the contents the way you want to—by keyword, client, industry, designer, style, or date, and even link to a designer's website or email.

This book delivers another sort of rich context, too: dozens of in-depth stories behind the birth of some of the most influential identity projects of our time. Travel through the back-story and the boardroom as designers weave through challenging obstacles to create visual identities for the likes of Sprint, the Beijing Olympics, Australia, AOL, Unilever, Bank of New York, and Target's private label Archer Farms, to name a few.

Why go to all this trouble? Because we think your time is important. The LogoLounge book series and website put inspiration at your fingertips in an instant so that you can spend more time designing and less time playing librarian for the creative universe.

—Bill Gardner

jurors

Emanuela Frigerio
C&G Partner, New York, NY

The Dog House logo, by DDB Dallas
"My favorite design is the The Dog House pet groom-ing logo. I love its simplicity. It is clear, memorable, and timeless—all the attributes a successful logo should have. Though it unmistakably communicates that this is a pet grooming service, it also suggests a business that is caring and professional. The form is pleasing, and the one-color black solution, while basic, is perfect. I have to admit, it even made me smile, which is a rare quality for a logo, indeed."

Born and educated in the *fulcro* of Italian fashion and industrial design, Emanuela Frigerio has worked in Lon-don, Milan, Tokyo, and New York. Clients have included IBM, Knoll, the Museum of Modern Art, the Library of Congress, the U.S. General Services Administration, the Rockefeller Foundation, Harry N. Abrams, Crane & Co., and the McNay Art Museum.

A 15-year principal at Chermayeff & Geismar, Inc., she designed a 352-page monograph called *designing* that covers 45 years of the firm's work. She is currently a principal at C&G Partners together with Steff Geiss-buhler, Keith Helmetag, and Jonathan Alger.

Connie Birdsall
Lippincott Mercer, New York, NY

Central Christian Church logo, by Mindspace
"I chose this logo because it engaged me and pulled me into the design on a couple of levels—initially, the sheer restraint and striking elegance of the forms, and then the beautiful discovery of the characters holding hands when you take that second look. Such a won-derfully simple design solution resonates so strongly on many levels: The cross symbolizes Christianity, the peo-ple forms represent the church, and the simple use of color communicates the conflict resolution aspect. You don't even need the words. Then, you just can't get it out of your mind. It's sticky and memorable, more signs of a really effective logo design. When a designer gets the execution of the elements just right from a formal graphic perspective and tells a compelling story, it's a real accomplishment. The overall impression of the logo projects a real sense of humanity that leaves me with a positive, hopeful, and uplifted feeling."

Connie Birdsall, creative director and senior partner at Lippincott Mercer, has spent 20 years creating global corporate and brand identity programs, marketing com-munications systems, information design, launch and

implementation programs, and brand management tools. She has led the creative development of branding programs in Asia, Europe, Latin America, and the United States for clients such as Samsung, Citigroup, IBM, Continental Airlines, and, most recently, the Bank of New York and SK Group in Korea. A member of the National Board of Directors of the American Institute of Graphic Arts (AIGA), Birdsall holds a BFA from the Kansas City Art Institute and an MFA from Cranbrook Academy of Art.

Graham Purnell
Cato Purnell Partners, Melbourne, Australia

Doglogic logo by Elephandt in the Room

"My choice is Doglogic. It made me laugh. The designer obviously understood the core of what had to be communicated and how to do it with style, intelligence, and humor. A great idea, well executed."

Graham Purnell is partner with Ken Cato in Cato Purnell Partners. Under his creative direction, the firm has acquired new clients in a range of industries both in Australia and overseas. After earning a master of art degree from the Royal College of Arts in London in 1984, Purnell worked as senior designer at Minale Tattersfield. He subsequently worked in Singapore with Batey Advertising as design director.

Purnell's work has appeared in many international design publications, including *D&AD, Graphic,* and *Design Downunder.* His work for Energex, Coles Farmland, Kraft, Nestlé Nescafé, Primelife, Royal Guidedogs Association, and Suncorp Metway, and many other clients has earned a number of awards for Cato Purnell Partners.

Miles Newlyn
London, England

Kathy Taylor/Acupuncture & Chinese Herbalist logo, by Kahn Design

"I selected Kathy Taylor/Acupuncture & Chinese Herbalist as my favorite. I liked it because it drew me in and made me feel comfortable with alternative medicine. It could be read a number of ways—I like that—but one that appealed was that of knowledge passed from generation to generation. Hands are notoriously difficult to use in logo design, whilst offering great symbolism. This logo used the element of a hand in a way that circumvented the inherent awkwardness, resolving in a beautifully contained shape. A delicate but potent touch."

Miles Newlyn is a renowned typographer, thinker, and designer. He has worked for the world's top branding agencies to create identities for some of the world's leading businesses. Newlyn applies his talents to custom type design as well as logo design and is known for pushing the boundaries of the corporate sector. He has designed many famous logos, including marks for Honda and Unilever, and is also known for helping clients break out of twentieth-century communications strategies and talk today's language of hyperindividualism. Cult designer David Carson describes him as a "type designer extraordinaire," but Newlyn says he simply "designs for people, not markets."

Thomas Vasquez
Brooklyn, NY

MetaCosmetic logo, by GRAF d'SIGN Creative Boutique
"Extremely attractive, the MetaCosmetic logo is curvaceous but not overweight, slender without being too thin. It exudes sexuality, has a timeless personal style, expresses originality of thought, reproduces well, is a bit mysterious, and has a sense of humor. But above all, it is smart—and because of that, beautiful. The main problem: It is only a logo."

Since starting his career in the early 1990s in Dallas, Texas, Thomas Vasquez has shaped the way ideas and voices are expressed for some of the world's best-known brands. He has worked with Ogilvy & Mather's Brand Integration Group, creating solutions for IBM, Miller Brewing Co., and Maxwell House, after which he moved to the production company Cyclops. There he created print design and advertising for Levi's, Jockey International, and Universal Music Group, as well as title design work for RCA, ABC, and NBC. He also led the team responsible for rebranding one of the world's most recognizable icons, Elvis Presley.

After leaving Cyclops in 2004, Vasquez began consulting as a freelance design director to advertising agencies: Ogilvy & Mather, BBDO, J. Walter Thompson, DDB, and Berlin-Cameron. He also freelances as an art director for the Sunday edition of the *New York Times*. Most recently, he was chosen by Deutsche Bank to participate in a three-month public art exhibition celebrating the International Book Fair in Frankfurt, Germany. Vasquez has lectured on the subject of branding and identity design, and his work has been published in just about every national and international book and periodical on graphic design and advertising.

Robert Matza
Landor Associates, New York, NY

Eléctrica Bahia, by Oficina de Diseño y Marketing
"Simple, clean, well-balanced positive and negative space, and timeless: all ingredients for a successful mark. The electrical plug is clear and an appropriate message for this company. I was surprised and pleased, at second glance, to discover the hidden letter E. I appreciate the honesty and lack of frivolous decorative noise."

As creative director of Landor Associates New York, Robert Matza brings more than 17 years of experience to his corporate identity clients. In addition to working closely with his design team, Matza collaborates with all other disciplines within the office, including naming, strategy, and new business marketing. Since joining Landor in 1997, he has directed identity programs for Morgan Stanley, GE, PepsiCo, Tenaris, Computer Associates, New York Stock Exchange, Vanguard Group, Lenovo, Cleveland Clinic, Verizon, and Nielsen Media Research. More recently, he built programs for Bristol-Myers Squibb, Citigroup, and IBM. Matza also serves as creative director of Klamath Communications,

a specialized group that delivers a full spectrum of integrated communications to select Landor clients.

Prior to joining Landor, Matza spent 4 years at Chermayeff & Geismar, where he worked with clients such as Sony Entertainment, Telemundo, Mobil Corporation, and Simon & Schuster. He has lived and worked in Madrid, Spain, and through client relationships in South America and Europe he has developed extensive international experience. He holds a BFA in Graphic Design from the Rhode Island School of Design and volunteers his time and services for many nonprofit organizations.

Kit Paul
Brandient, Bucharest, Romania

Canadian Museum for Human Rights — Winnipeg, for Ralph Appelbaum Associates, by Polemic Design
"This is a piece of work I really admire. The designer achieved a groundbreaking effect by understated, almost humble means, cleverly embedding right into the logo the value this brand stands for: the belief that human rights always come first. Also, I've never seen such a dramatic representation of the truth in Victor Papanek's statement that 'design is the conscious effort to impose a meaningful order'—my favorite definition of design seen from quite a literal, unexpected angle."

Cristian "Kit" Paul is a founding partner and creative director of Brandient, the Romanian brand strategy and design consultancy. Before setting up the consultancy with his partners, he cut his teeth on many advertising campaigns and won coveted national and international nominations and prizes while working as an art director and creative director with the advertising agencies Graffiti/BBDO, Tempo, and D'Arcy DMB&B in Bucharest. He also worked as a freelance graphic designer in Romania and Singapore. Presently, Paul is deeply rooted in corporate identity while publicly advocating the role of design.

HUMAN RIGHTS CANADIAN MUSEUM FOR

Sharon Werner
Werner Design Werks, Minneapolis, MN

Mjólka logo, by Ó!
"Smart, simple, memorable, cute. What more could you ask?"

Sharon Werner founded the Minneapolis-based design firm Werner Design Werks, Inc., in 1991. The small studio specializes in combining strong visual language with sound design solutions to create work that affects not only commerce but culture. The office has worked with Target Corporation, Mohawk Paper, Chronicle Books, Mrs. Meyer's Clean Day, Blu Dot Design and Manufacturing, Nick at Nite, VH1 Networks, Levi's, Minnesota Public Radio, and Moët Hennessy.

Werner's office has garnered national and international awards and honors, and was named the Target Corporation's Vendor of the Year in 2002. WDW's work is included in *100 World's Best Posters* and is part of the permanent collection of the Library of Congress, the Rumpus Room of Ernest and Viola Werner, Musée de la Poste, Victoria and Albert Museum, Musée des Arts Décoratifs, and the Cooper Hewitt Museum.

portraits

Design Firm	Desgrippes Gobé
Client	America Online
Project	Corporate Identity Redesign

In 2003, America Online was becoming increasingly irrelevant to consumers, and in more than a few instances it was referenced as "training wheels for the Internet," especially as consumers were moving quickly from dial-up to broadband access.

"In truth, AOL was one of the first proponents of high-speed connections. But consumers did not relate that to AOL," notes Marc Gobé, principal and chief creative officer for Desgrippes Gobé, New York City, the design firm that undertook the rebranding for the online giant. "The company needed a new image and message in order to change perceptions."

> It was really important to show AOL's commitment to society.

In its early days, America Online worked hard to dispel the fears many people had about using the Internet—indeed, about using computers at all. Its friendly, helpful image (like that of a cheerful primary school teacher) resonated with users. As the company moved into broadband and wireless and added high-tech services, however, it had to confront newcomers such as MSN and Yahoo.

America Online did have one powerful attribute that the others did not: a tremendous emotional connection with customers.

"Historically, AOL is like a friend with a comforting nature. It gets people on the Internet in an easy way. We needed to move from that into a position of being a savvy, trusted partner. AOL offers products and services that are innovative and smart, but it also offers security and protection for families. It was really important to show their commitment to society," Gobé explains.

Desgrippes Gobé worked with the AOL brand strategy team to ensure that the new visual identity was aligned with a new positioning that focuses on fighting for the consumer. This focus is now echoed in the tagline, "Want a better Internet?"

Regaining a leadership position while maintaining that emotional relationship—a relationship critical to customer loyalty—would be a tricky proposition. Gobé says the new positioning had to demonstrate that the service was on the customer's side, looking out for him or her and truly caring about the online experience.

(Above left) Desgrippes Gobé gave AOL's logo an interesting new slant—literally. When the old logo was turned just slightly, it became an arrow pointing AOL users to the future.

(Above right) AOL's logo was familiar to anyone on the Internet—too familiar, in fact. It had become such an integral feature of the cyberspace skyscape that it was almost invisible.

AOL's new three-dimensional logo is brought to life in an innovative CD package that reinforces the shape whenever the customer comes into contact with it. The case was also used as a 3-D graphic in retail displays (right).

Changing the triangle into an arrow transformed the logo from a marker to a message.

Degrippes Gobé also designed an AOL experiential store in New York City that turned the brand into a sensory experience. It contains a sound studio where people can listen to music and an electronic bar with computers for sending email or photos taken in the store. Some of the photos were used to build a mosaic of faces. "In sharing your face, you were showing you were part of a much larger community. A huge part of the Internet is a sense of community," explains DGA principal Marc Gobé.

We float in space and have the freedom to reach new dimensions. This logo also lives in space.

There is some danger in changing a familiar logo, he notes. On the other hand, when a logo becomes too familiar, it loses its meaning and becomes, essentially, invisible.

The original AOL triangle mark had value as a recognizable shape, but it had faded into the background of cyberspace. Gobé wanted to transform it into something new: with a slight tilt, the triangle could be turned into an arrow pointing forward into the future.

"We did not have to stick with the triangle, but the shape had such awareness among the company's 20-million-plus users. Current and past AOL members consistently recalled two elements of the current logo as key to what AOL stands for—the color blue and the triangle. Changing it into an arrow transformed the logo from a marker to a message," the designer says.

The arrow announced the company's commitment to guiding users to new experiences and continually providing new features and services while preserving the core, recognizable elements of AOL—its warmth and optimism.

In the original logo, the triangle contains two swirls moving in a closed circle. Here, the circle is transformed into a globe, an intuitive symbol of the benefits of the Internet: a roundtable where people come together; a circular,

never-ending power source; a trackball the user can always control; or even the center of the online universe around which new experiences orbit.

Gobé also gave the logo a three-dimensional quality, with rounded corners and corresponding highlights, which lifts it off of the background. Rounding the corners on the logo and the letterforms was critical to aligning the logo with the positioning—it's not about AOL, it's about the consumer.

"This is appropriate particularly when you consider that we live in a wireless society. We float in space and have the freedom to reach new dimensions. This logo also lives in space. It was a signal that the brand was moving into a new era," he adds.

Typography was updated with simple, light letterforms that convey warmth and modernity. The resulting signature is clean and well defined, and it stands out from competing logos on the Internet and in media space.

The finished logo projects the sense that AOL is the place where everything connects. It is the trailhead from which new experiences can be explored.

"It invites you in and takes you to different place," says Gobé.

Travelocity
Identity Design

Desgrippes Gobé, New York, New York

Like America Online, Travelocity was an early leader in its field—in its case, online travel planning. But before long, competitors such as Orbitz and Expedia began to infringe on its territory.

"Travelocity forgot that they were not in the technology business or simply providing tickets to people: They were in the business of providing dreams," says Desgrippes Gobé principal Marc Gobé.

Travelocity had a special edge that the others did not, however. Rather than simply list or describe a possible destination, the company actually sent representatives there to audit the location for specific criteria. The information the site provided was not a canned sales speech but rather a description that actually analyzed the destination.

This unique service gave customers a sense of trust in the company. Gobé wanted to build on that wedge. What was missing, however, was a real emotional connection to the brand. The old logo certainly didn't have it; its chartlike design could easily be mistaken for a financial group's mark.

Gobé's team began with an internal brainstorming session with Travelocity managers. The outcome was clear: Every person there had a real passion for the brand. They truly wanted it to be the best place for people to begin what would turn into wonderful travel experiences. The old brand did not speak of dreams or freedom or any of the things travelers anticipate.

The designers began by considering symbolism that would suggest dreams. The notion of wishing on a star—or wishing on many stars—emerged as a strong favorite.

"From an emotional perspective, we wanted the new logo to be more about possibilities. We wanted it to suggest that it can help you transcend your normal life. So we needed to express a sense of magic, discovery, imagination, freedom, and limitless boundaries," Gobé says.

The team's solution was a trio of loosely brushstroked stars. The hand-drawn effect makes the new logo more personal and friendly. Its simple nature complements the typography, which includes the company's slogan. Sans-serif type also feels friendly and approachable.

For color, the designers chose blue to signify open skies and orange to communicate energy. "Orange is an optimistic color," Gobé notes. "It's a transformative color, associated with the sun, so it is warm and glowing."

When used in reverse, the stars glow in white. "They give you the feeling you get when you lay down in a field at night: You can spend hours just looking at the sky and its mystery," he adds.

Working in tandem with Travelocity's new "spokes-gnome," the new logo literally changed the face of the business. The entire site adopted the same spirit as the logo. It is now more about discovery as opposed to just plopping information in front of the reader.

"The new identity reflects the desire of company employees to do a better job for people. It really shows their sincerity," the designer says.

Design Firm	Armstrong International CI
Client	2008 Olympics Committee
Project	Logo Design

The 2008 Beijing Olympics committee received 1,985 entries in response to its logo competition invitation, issued in 2002. Of these, 1,763 were from designers in China, Taiwan, and Hong Kong. Among the entries was work by designers who had won the logo competitions for the 1996 Atlanta Olympics, the 1998 Nagano Winter Olympics, the 2000 Sydney Olympics, and the 2002 Salt Lake City Winter Olympics.

Against this stiff competition, a design by Guo Chunning, president of Armstrong International Corporate Identity Design Co., Ltd. stood out. His logo portrays a running, celebrating figure—perfectly appropriate to the Games—but it has a distinct Chinese sensibility, plus plenty of hidden meaning.

> It has been more than 100 years since the Olympics were born, and now they have finally come to Beijing.

Among countries that might host the Olympics, China's history and culture are especially ancient and rich. It has many, many stories to share with the world. Creating a logo that picked out just the right stories and combining those with the spirit of the Olympics was challenging, says Guo.

"That was the problem we had to solve first," he says. "It has been more than 100 years since the Olympics were born, and now they finally come to Beijing. This is such a big honor."

Guo wanted to create a symbol that not only could be appreciated in nations and cultures around the world but also in the many subcultures of his own country.

"There were many, many cultural inheritances and artistic elements to consider—for instance, calligraphy, sculpture, silk, fresco, pottery and porcelain, religious art, folk art, and architectural arts. There were so many elements for us to choose from," he says.

After long consideration, Guo chose Chinese calligraphy and seal cutting. Still in use today, seal cutting is an ancient art that dates back 3,700 years. A seal is essentially a stamped signature produced intaglio with a carefully carved and thoughtfully designed stamp.

(Above) The logo for the 2008 Beijing Olympics was created by a Beijing design firm, Armstrong International Corporate Identity Design Co., Ltd. The design is built on the ancient Chinese art of seal cutting and on an actual Chinese character.

(Right) The design team began their explorations with this Chinese character, pronounced "jing." It means "Beijing," which is certainly appropriate, but in addition, the designers could see in it a human form that was running or leaping.

BEIJING 2008

(Above) The logo the team submitted to the Olympics Committee for consideration is basic in form. Because it uses red, the color traditionally used in the art of seal cutting, it has the appearance of a traditional seal cut stamp to those familiar to the art— generally, the Chinese host citizens. However, it also speaks to those who are not familiar with seal cutting.

(Right) The Olympic Committee asked that the Armstrong designers try out several typefaces. Traditional Western faces as well as Chinese brush-inspired faces were explored.

Combining the figure and the color in the cutting turned it into an official seal of sorts.

(Top) Here, the character is modified to appear as if it is running or leaping. The sense of the Chinese character is still present, however. The trial at far right shows a child-lettered design; Armstrong asked 300 children to hand-write the words *Beijing 2008* in an attempt to capture a more unfettered spirit. Although they were appealing, none were chosen.

(Bottom) In this version, the running character changed yet again, although the type-face has been chosen: a sim-plified Chinese brush style.

送审方案之一

送审方案之二

送审方案之三

送审方案之一

送审方案之二

送审方案之三

送审方案之四

Guo and Armstrong chairman Zhang Wu also considered the relative success and appropriateness of logos from previous Games. Zhang felt that designs from the 1984, 1992, and 2004 Olympics were particularly successful.

Each Olympics logo represents the host country's culture and artistic characteristic, says Guo. He wanted Armstrong's logo to do the same, and more.

He began his design by selecting a Chinese character, pronounced "jing," meaning Beijing. This character is a very basic one, and through careful thought and experimentation, the designer was able to transform it into a pictograph of a running figure. To Guo, the figure represented the spirit of the Olympics: faster, higher, stronger.

The figure represented the spirit of the Olympics: faster, higher, stronger.

"It is like a dancer waving his arms, welcoming friends from all over the world. It represents the new Beijing, a passionate Beijing, and an energetic Beijing," he says.

Guo decided to portray the figure in a seal cutting, which speaks of China's ancient culture and art. The color for seal cutting is red, which also happens to be the color of happiness and festival in the country. Combining the figure and the color in the cutting turned it into an official seal of sorts, but a seal that anyone around the world could understand. It made both the letterform and the art form universally understandable.

Selecting an appropriate typeface was a challenge. First, Guo tried a recognizable face, Times New Roman, as well as the face Chinese Brush. But neither of these had the same unfettered nature of Chinese calligraphy. So the design team invited 300 children to write, in their own handwriting, the words *Beijing 2008*. None of these trials was an ideal match, however, so finally Guo decided to use simplified Chinese brushstroked characters, which the Olympics committee praised.

The mark, called "Dancing Beijing," was released for use in 2003, and Zhang Wu and Guo are pleased with its life thus far.

"It is like my dream coming true," says Guo. "It was really hard to express my feelings in words at that time. I felt so proud that our Chinese design was well accepted by the world. This is a honor for my company, my country, and the Chinese designers."

The logo, called "Dancing Beijing," was released for use in 2003, and it now appears not only in Olympic and other athletic applications but also in signage and other graphics in its host city.

China National Petroleum Corporation
Identity Design

Armstrong International CI, Beijing, China

The old logo of the China National Petroleum Corporation certainly did not reflect either the scope or the energy of the state holding company's main products, crude oil and natural gas. An oval, split lengthwise into yellow and red, featured the letters CNPC at its center.

There was little contrast between the letterforms and the yellow half of the logo, and that contrast all but disappeared when the logo was used small. When shown in combination with product logos from its own lines, it did not stand out. The company, which ranks forty-sixth in the Fortune Global 500 list, clearly needed a more distinctive identity.

CNPC asked Armstrong International Corporate Identity Design Co., Ltd. in Beijing, China, to build up its global image. To accomplish this, Armstrong director Zhang Wu and his team wanted to draw from the far more recognizable logo of a CNPC product, Kunlan lubricating oil.

"Kunlan Mountain is one of the most famous mountains in China. It has witnessed the development of Chinese civilization and is a significant visual element of Chinese civilization," says Zhang Wu.

The design team's solution combined the shape of the mountain with a rising sun, also a meaningful symbol in China, to form a round droplet shape. "It is like an oil drop, representing the ambition of CNPC," the director explains. "It represents never-ending energy, the motto of CNPC—'Dedication to the energy industry, building the harmony'—the relationship between CNPC and the [Chinese] people, and between CNPC and nature."

Maintaining the original color scheme made sense: The colors are warm, consistent with the company's dedication to building harmony, and red and yellow are the colors of the Chinese national flag. While yellow was ineffective as a background for letters in the original logo, it works well as a backdrop to a rising sun.

The new logo has been well received, and it is quickly being disseminated inside and outside the country. It has traveled to Antarctica with a Chinese team of researchers sponsored by CNPC. In addition, the corporation is an official sponsor of the 2008 Beijing Olympics, so its new identity will soon be visible to people worldwide.

Design Firm	Lippincott Mercer
Client	Bank of New York
Project	Corporate Identity Redesign

A client with a 200-year history also has 200 years' worth of identity, for better or for worse. That's what Lippincott Mercer discovered when it began to excavate the brand identity of the Bank of New York.

The Bank of New York's logo—a safe burgundy box with white type inside—had been a regional icon, long recognizable in the New York area but uninspiring just the same. In the mid-1990s, the Bank embarked on a ten-year string of acquisitions. More than eighty acquisitions later, the bank had vastly broadened its capabilities in custody, trade execution and clearing, corporate trust, and institutional asset management. No longer a regional entity, the Bank needed to be reintroduced to the world.

> A big part of reintroducing the Bank of New York, which was founded by Alexander Hamilton, was implementing a new identity.

"Founded by Alexander Hamilton, the Bank of New York is America's oldest bank. In fact, it was the first bank in the colonies to create currency," explains Alex de Janosi, lead designer for the project at Lippincott Mercer. "It has an incredibly rich history. But it has grown considerably in the last fifteen to twenty-five years. Today, it moves a trillion dollars a day."

The Bank has always had a large retail footprint, but customers, both individuals and corporate entities, did not realize how much it had changed. Even Bank of New York employees did not fully understand the new scope. The Bank had become a leading provider of financial services on an international level. A big part of reintroducing the financial giant was implementing a new identity.

"The Bank's old logo was very drab, very dated. It was nothing horrible, but certainly nothing evocative," explains de Janosi. Trite images of globes, meant to suggest a global presence, also figured prominently in Bank promotions. Most collateral materials were printed on uninspiring cream-colored stock.

Even more troublesome, the burgundy box logo was used inconsistently. "Every line of business that the Bank of New York had could do whatever it wanted. Everything was disparate and not uniform. We needed to make 'the Bank of New York' the brand here, not the company's different offerings and products."

(Above) The Bank of New York's new logo, designed by Lippincott Mercer, radiates the power and dynamism of the organization while quietly noting its 200-year history.

(Right) The client's old logo was safe but uninspiring and even drab in many applications. In addition, the Bank's many divisions used the identity inconsistently.

The new mark is embossed for special applications, such as executive business cards.

Color and pattern make the Bank of New York's new logo an enormous leap forward in terms of presence in the market. The patterning in the logo references traditional patterning in currency and financial certificates, while the colors suggest the modern world and its energetic pace. The empty center of the new mark could even be regarded as a subtle mimic of the original square mark.

The logo isn't a beauty mark; it has to convey specific attributes.

Lippincott Mercer's job was threefold:

- Organize the Bank's many divisions, business, and offerings so future marketing efforts could be integrated.

- Create a new marketing platform.

- Create a new identity program that, at a glance, helps customers understand the Bank of New York.

Lippincott Mercer began the project by interviewing the Bank's key audiences, including banking professionals, employees, clients, and financial analysts, to better understand wider perceptions of the brand, especially in relation to how competitors (such as State Street, Mellon, and JP Morgan Chase) were regarded.

After a year of research, the design team identified a clear set of brand attributes, which included descriptors such as *responsive, industry leader,* and *global.*

"As designers, we don't put pencil to paper until the attributes are agreed upon. The logo isn't a beauty mark; it has to convey specific attributes," de Janosi says.

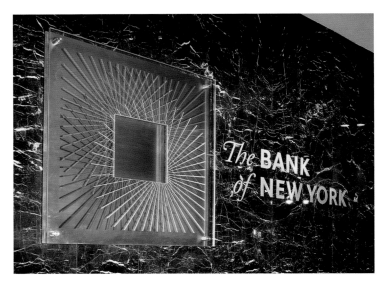

The levels of radiating lines in the mark are especially useful in dimensional applications, such as this signage.

> To balance the bright colors and flowing lines, the team crafted solid, stable typography.

Eight designers then began creating a broad range of symbols and logotypes. This marked a surprisingly lengthy phase of the project. Nearly six months passed, during which the client even considered abandoning the Bank of New York name.

During the exploration process, the designers looked at images of Alexander Hamilton's financial motifs, graphic patterns and shapes, and straight typographic expressions.

The design team met with the project director to narrow the hundreds of marks to a list of ten ideas to present to the Bank's chairman.

The designers had discovered shapes and overlapping lines that resembled engraving patterns on historic stock certificates and global currencies. The intertwining lines suggested the Bank's comprehensive and integrated array of services.

The response by the client was favorable. "They really liked the idea of graphics that expressed transactions, management, and movement of money," de Janosi says.

When an early sample of the patterning concept was shown together with other ideas, the Bank of New York chair and other members of top management rallied around it. The ebb and flow of the linear patterning spoke to the Bank's technical abilities. The introduction of transparent colors gave the mark a fresh, modern look while conveying an established, elegant feel, plus the square shape of the design subtly referenced the shape of the old logo.

To balance the bright colors and flowing lines, de Janosi's team crafted solid, stable typography. The logotype, a combination of the fonts Bliss and Adobe Garamond, was carefully customized: Ligatures between the *T* and *he* as the elegant italic of *the* and *of* represent the history of the brand. The elegant gray of the type balances well with the vibrant linework in the mark, nicely mixing history with modernity.

The visual equity of the original logo's box was maintained. The shape is called "the jewel box." It is as if the original burgundy box were opened and all the colorful workings of the company revealed. The shape of the box is echoed in the design grid used in many other applications today— the Bank's website, signage, and more.

De Janosi and his team worked many hours making certain that the line weights involved with the jewel box were appropriate and that lines inside related to the bounding box correctly. Of course, there were many production aspects to consider with the fine lines and choice of colors.

"With a five-color logo, anything can get mangled in the wrong hands. But the internal marketing staff at the Bank runs a tight ship, and they keep a close eye on how people use the jewel box. It's an ongoing job."

Although at the start of the project, the Bank of New York had many fiefdoms that each had a strong opinion about the company's identity and its use. Today, the many divisions have embraced the new look and philosophy.

The Bank of New York's new look is a definite swing away from the past as well as a shift away from the personality of competitors. It's even more successful than de Janosi originally believed it might be.

"The culture of the previous identity was weighed down with yellow-cream paper, burgundy boxes, and so on. I was surprised at senior management's excitement over the new mark, which we presented as a real long shot. They were all over it," he recalls. "The lesson for me is to not underestimate a client's tastes or capabilities. The client can see beauty and function just the same as you do."

(Top) The shape of the new logo drives a grid system that is easily adaptable for collateral design.

(Bottom) Because of its mix of modern and traditional, the new logo is extremely flexible. It can be used in applications small and large.

Sprint
Identity Design

Lippincott Mercer, New York, New York

The goal in developing a new identity for the company formed by the 2005 merger of Sprint and Nextel was to retain valuable visual equities from each company yet move on to a stronger, even more valuable positioning. Even though the new company would be named Sprint, its new management team did not want to suggest that one company was overpowering the other. This was to be a real merger.

"We wanted to explore the 'Sprintness' and 'Nextelness' the identity needed, as well as the ramifications for creating something in a completely new direction," explains Rodney Abbot, senior partner at Lippincott Mercer (New York City), the design and brand consultancy that developed the new Sprint logo. "We had to retain what was valuable from both brands and move forward, not just move on."

The original Sprint organization had come to own such concepts as clarity—as portrayed by the famous pin drop—as well as dynamism and the heritage of a friendly communications business. Nextel owned the color combination of yellow and black in the communications market. Combined with a direct, no-nonsense attitude, its original logo felt solid and technologically strong.

Abbot and his design team developed many directions. Some stayed close to the original identities, while others signaled a complete break from the past. All the designs were created to convey the key brand qualities of choice, flexibility, clarity, immediacy, directness, and straight talk.

"We wanted to visually express the experience the customer would have, regardless of whether the customer is a business or personal use customer," says Abbot. The new logo had to communicate the company's appropriate connection to home and business.

As their design work progressed, the team noted that the most emotional responses from focus groups were garnered from simple, direct, strong shapes, those that had a dynamic sense of movement and a distinct personality. The final design captured those qualities and expressed them in a new design reminiscent of a wing. It has a quality of flight, freedom, and movement, especially when it is run in the familiar Nextel yellow.

"It also has a sense of moving forward," Abbot says. "It indicates a transformation in the communication experience you will have with the new brand."

For the type, the designers selected a sans serif that felt fresher and more responsive than the Garamond Italic used in the old Sprint logo and the heavy sans used in the old Nextel logo. Open letterspacing allows the new symbol to fly untethered.

Design Firm	**FutureBrand**
Client	**Brand Australia**
Project	**Corporate Identity Redesign**

No one would deny that Australia is an exotic, fantastic vacation destination. Trouble is, it's quite a hike from just about everywhere else in the world: A traveler makes a considerable effort to get there. Given, in addition, the SARS scare in Southeast Asia and the general nervous malaise caused by terrorism worldwide, visits to Australia declined in 2003.

At that time, the Australian Tourism Commission decided to refresh the country's tourism identity and rejuvenate travelers' interest. The commission itself was rebranded as Tourism Australia, and the new group came to FutureBrand with a challenging brief.

> **The goal: Create a 360-degree view of Australia by aligning key ideas and messages across policy, trade, and travel channels.**

First, they wanted to refresh Brand Australia's visual image and create a 360-degree view of Australia by aligning key ideas and messages across policy, trade, and travel channels. The new identity had to establish a comprehensive brand strategy that would help partners like Qantas, the Australian airline, and state tourism authorities work in a more complementary way. Finally, the new identity system had to be flexible so that partners—in tourism, education, trade, and politics—could enjoy success through the use of the same smart branding tools.

"The client's old identity did not reflect how Australia had emerged as a major destination. There is a rich, deep story here to be told," explains Ken Shadbolt, creative director of FutureBrand's Melbourne office.

Shadbolt's designers were presented with a brief informed by New York–based brand consultancy Brand Architecture International:

• The Australian experience is bright, literally and figuratively, which cultivates a pervasive and infectious candor and optimism.

• It is a place that lives in the future tense, always looking and creating forward, where time is always now.

• Australia is a place refreshingly free of boundaries, inhibitions, and constraints, where "having a go" is still possible.

(Above) Show Australia in a different light—that was the goal of the FutureBrand team in designing a new identity for Australia.com. The jumping kangaroo, the distinctive typeface and color palette, indigenous patterning, and, perhaps most distinctive, the glow or flare or spark of the sun all play an important part of the design solution.

(Right) The old identity spoke clearly of sun, sea, and life native to Australia, but it was somewhat uninspiring and flat. It did not tell the viewer anything about the experiences he or she might have there.

- It is a place where blue-sky thinking is the rule, not the exception.

- It is a place in which one cannot help but be irreverent, to approach things from unexpected angles, to see things through different lenses.

"A different light" was a leading factor from the start of the project, says Shadbolt. The concept referred to the actual physical quality of the light in Australia as well as the country's sense of can-do energy and optimism. "People often comment when they step off a plane that they are quite struck by the intensity of light, its vibrancy," he says. "We wanted to capture that vibrancy as well as the effect it has on all living things that are touched by it."

The challenge for the FutureBrand team was to find a way to express visually this physical and emotional light. Their ideas came from many sources. They looked at photos that contained evocative light phenomena, such as sunbursts, flares, reflections on water, refraction, and backlighting. Because of the country's reputation for wonderful sun and water, these could all be used in the new identity.

Any photography used as part of the identity, they decided, should deliberately avoid typical tourist shots. Many of the images in the previous photographic library showed beautiful landscapes at sunset, but they were all shot with the sun behind the photographer. "We wanted to challenge that predictable approach," says Shadbolt. Instead, the FutureBrand team decided to commission photography from a more unusual angle—directly into the sun—making the images considerably more distinctive.

Vibrant light inspiration also came from the charged strokes of contemporary indigenous art. "The living line," the designers called it, as it is full of shimmering dots and swirling shapes that are full of energy and indeed, history. Lines, they reasoned, could symbolize feelings and patterns of energy.

"Bringing these graphics to the fore of this identity system was very important," says Shadbolt. "We commissioned an indigenous group—Balarinji, based in Sydney—to create this artwork. We briefed them to explore art that expressed emotional states, such as calmness or adventure. We were so excited when the work came back. The extraordinary connection between the land and the people who live here is beautifully expressed by this artwork."

(Above) The colors and patterning of Australian indigenous art play an important part in the finished identity. The graphical patterning can be run over photos or used as dividers or incidental art.

(Below) The designers created a palette of five colors, each with two shades—one as the color appears in full sun and one as it appears in shade. Some combinations were lively, suggesting adventure. Others were more grounded to suggest the rest and peace travelers also desire from a vacation destination. All the colors emerged from the native surroundings of the country.

The colors used in the indigenous art, photography, and other applications were crucial to the identity's success. The designers built a distinctive palette of five colors, each with two shades—one as the color appears in full sun, the other as it appears in shadow. Some could be used in what they called "irreverent combinations" to suggest the excitement of travel and adventure. Others made more "grounded" pairs, perfect for representing the peace and quiet space travelers also seek from their experiences abroad.

Two contrasting typefaces were selected for the project. FutureBrand worked with the Font Bureau to customize an existing hand-drawn font for brief applications, such as headlines and call-outs, that can have more personality. These typefaces were complemented by a relaxed and straightforward sans-serif font used for informational text.

> We decided to work with the roo—it was pretty much a given. However, the way we represented it had to be very distinctive.

Two new fonts were created for a hand-drawn and casual look. One is used for short applications, such as headlines, and one for informational text, as shown here.

The kangaroo might be an Australian cliché, but it is so firmly connected to the country that it is impossible to ignore. The key to using it smartly is to give it special life and energy, just like the country itself. These are just a few of the roos that auditioned for the starring role in the identity.

The design team carefully studied what competing tourist destinations, such as Hawaii, Brazil, Japan, Spain, Malaysia, New Zealand, and others, were doing. They also considered the recognizable icons of Australia, including the kangaroo from the original identity.

"From an Australian perspective, the kangaroo is a bit of a cliché. Most of us are so affected by clichés that we immediately want to get rid of them. However, when you think about someone in another part of the world who is considering five to ten possible locations to visit, we have to cut through quickly with our message. The unique shape of the kangaroo carries considerable equity of Australia," says Shadbolt. "The old version of the kangaroo was quite tired. As we were reminded of many times during this identity refresh, there are no tired icons, just tired expressions."

The kangaroo, in addition to building on existing equity (within the commission and with businesses such as Qantas) and being a highly recognizable icon, is also a living creature with the same irrepressible spirit that the new commission wanted to express. The animal in the previous logo seemed to be on a downward trajectory. For the new logo, the designers experimented with showing the kangaroo on an upward journey. Many drawings also showed a sun with just a suggestion of a smile.

Their final design includes the leaping animal, a sun drawn in a loose style, colors that sweep from high noon to dusk, spirited typography, and a sunburst or flare of light.

"We decided to work with the roo—it was pretty much a given. However, the way we represented it had to be distinctive. We made it come alive with the light. The light gets in and affects you. The spirit can't be dormant here," says Shadbolt.

An additional benefit of the new logo and identity system is that it is very flexible: all of its components can be mixed and matched in endless combinations. For instance, a pattern can be used alone on top of color, or it can serve as a transitional element between a block of solid color and a photo. A pattern can be overlaid on a photo, which always yields a wonderful play of light and people. The emphasis is on demonstrating that the Australian experience involves much more than just seeing icons. It is about feeling the whole of the place.

Implemented in May 2004, the new system is being credited with an increase in attention. At the end of December 2004, international tourist traffic into Australia was up 9 percent from the previous year, and it increased by a further 7 percent in the nine months to September 2005.

The Brand Council in the United Kingdom has named Australia as one of the world's Cool BrandLeaders, especially interesting as this is the first time a country was included on this annual list. Additionally, in November 2005 Australia was awarded the title of "best worldwide country," by readers of the *Sunday Times* Travel Magazine in the United Kingdom.

"Our brand identity work has played its part in communicating Brand Australia more clearly and consistently around the world," says Shadbolt, "so it's hard to argue with the notion that multidimensional brands like countries really benefit from careful thought in the expression of their offer."

"Our job was to inspire tourism, but this identity also affects other areas of trade. Other Australian organizations are looking at leveraging the new identity in a much broader role internationally. One possibility is that, over time, it will become the national brand," says Shadbolt.

Australia has many well photographed sites and sights. Rather than rely on these alone, as so many did before, the designers decided to add two more elements: the unusual quality of light presented by the Australian sun, and the human element. The latter helps viewers imagine themselves in the picture. In the samples above, indigenous patterning is also played over the photo, enhancing the sense of the fantastic. In the samples at right, patterning is used in combination with color as a graphic divider.

The new logo and identity system is enormously flexible. Color, light, fonts, patterns, and photos can be combined in endless ways.

More samples of printed pieces. Note how the distinctive quality of light shines through in each photo and how patterning adds layer, dimension, and personality to the other elements.

2006 Commonwealth Games
Identity Design

FutureBrand, Melbourne, Australia

Like the Olympic Games, the Common-wealth Games bring together talented athletes and enthusiastic fans every four years. Also like the Olympic Games, the Commonwealth Games have a different host city and different logo and identity each time they are held. Unlike the Olympic Games, though, the Commonwealth Games are open only to countries in the British Commonwealth, which makes them a much more intimate event. Without the power countries that tend to dominate the Olympic Games, many more Commonwealth athletes have a chance to demonstrate their personal best.

FutureBrand Melbourne, which designed the identity for the 2000 Summer Olympic Games in Sydney, Australia, had clear ideas about where it wanted to take the 2006 Commonwealth Games logo. Past logos had a strong British flavor: in fact, right into the 1970s and 1980s, they almost all contained a reference to the Union Jack. The past marks also felt formal, with no sense of the celebration and thrill the athletes and audiences experience.

"We really wanted to cut free of the British ties," explains Ken Shadbolt, creative director of FutureBrand. "It is the games of the Commonwealth, but what is the relevance of that to the games today? For us, it meant the notion of diverse backgrounds and origins, but of shared values."

At the outset of the project, the FutureBrand team discovered it would have to incorporate the Commonwealth Federation logo—just created—into the Games logo. Having worked with the

MELBOURNE
2006
XVIII COMMONWEALTH GAMES
TM©

Olympic rings, the designers knew that the federation mark would have to be prominent despite its lack of graphic inspiration.

Unlike Sydney, Melbourne does not have physical icons that are recognized worldwide, which was an additional complication. The city does, however, have a cultural sophistication the designers felt they could express visually. The new logo could be a celebration of sport and culture together.

"These games are all about youthful optimism and sportsmanship, but more about taking part than winning. We wanted to communicate a sense of celebration beyond the sport, because actually, many cultural events run concurrently to the games. So the new symbol would have to represent those experiences as well," says Shadbolt.

The solution expresses the spirit of athleticism and celebration, of diverse origins and colors, and of sharing. Two figures mesh, one striving and one celebrating, and together form a hint of an M. This logo celebrates winning not just through actual victory but through sportsmanship and experience as well.

Shadbolt feels the new logo raises the excitement of the event several notches and will give future designers expanded license in future logo designs. The project will open up over time, and, like the Olympic Games, give both future athletes and designers splendid opportunities.

Design Firm	Wolff Olins
Client	Beeline
Project	Corporate Identity System

The cell and mobile phone market is growing explosively around the world, including Russia, where a number of providers are already in place. The number-two player in early 2005 was Beeline, a brand that had been in existence since 1993. Beeline had the same serious business problem as other providers: a sizable hole in its client loyalty quotient. Seventy percent of Muscovites use cell phones, and most were selecting their cell service strictly on the basis of price. They were easily distracted by newer and cheaper options.

Brand loyalty—and, indeed, the concept of a brand—was little known. Beeline wanted to find a way to secure an invaluable emotional tie to their customers: it needed a recognizable brand.

> Brand loyalty—and, indeed, the concept of a brand—was little known at Beeline.

Beeline's competition, which included MTC and Megaphone, was tough, but Beeline had the benefit of an already well-recognized logo, which contained a bee. The old logo represented the brand name in Cyrillic letters, with the image of the bee between "Bee" and "line" against a blue background. It was a naïve but compelling and friendly icon, something the creative team at Wolff Olins, which was asked to create the new brand, could build around.

The Wolff Olins creative team was asked to keep the heritage bumblebee in the final design solution. It carried some brand equity and had a real sense of life. Moreover, because bees are known for building communities, collaborating, and communicating, the image held particular relevance for the client.

But the designers considered a less literal take on the bee. Rather than include the image of an actual bee in the new logo, they decided to appropriate its yellow and black striped pattern.

"We wanted to give Beeline something they could own and play with graphically—something recognizable, free, and inspiring," explains Marina Willer, Wolff Olins creative director for the project.

The striped pattern became a theme that could be applied to almost anything—clothing, objects, even other animals. Some of Willer's favorite applications have been a zebra and ice cream: "Because they twist

(Above) Wolff Olins designers took the identity of the cell phone company Beeline from drab to full of personality and color. The new logo stands out by virtue of its simplicity.

(Right) Beeline's original logo suggested energy and communication, but its main character, the bee, did not have much life. Amid the cacophony of talk and marketing that surrounds the competitive Russian cell phone market, it just did not stand out.

escape

create

Rather than play out Beeline's new logo over and over, the Wolff Olins design team applied the mark's distinctive color scheme to everyday objects that suggested inspirational messages such as escape or relax. As these signboards show, neither the logo nor the company name must be shown to communicate the brand.

play

live life

dream

relax

ordinary images that people are familiar with into something extraordinary, that treatment makes them Beeline and nothing else."

Yellow is an energetic, warm color, and this quality made the new identity appealing to Russians. "With the weather and history there, Russia can be a tough place to live. It's almost surreal. I think people are desperate for sun and warmth. The contrast with black is quite brutal, but it works there. Subtlety is something that would just not work," Willer says.

> We wanted to provide a breath of fresh air with plenty of white space.

When Wolff Olins began working with Beeline in mid-2005, the idea of a branded experience was not widely known in Russia. "The notion of a consistent brand across several media is new in Russia," says Willer. "Big cities like Moscow have a busy, noisy landscape. Everything is big, and there is a lot of noise pollution. Everyone is shouting their marketing message at the same volume. It really is a brutal landscape."

A metropolitan city like London or New York City is also quite loud, she notes, but these cities regulate and limit the size and placement of

billboards and other visual media. Russian cities have no such rules. This environment was quite a concern for the design team when they first arrived. How could Beeline even begin to be noticed?

"That's when we decided to do something quite simple. We wanted to provide a breath of fresh air with plenty of white space," says Willer.

All of Beeline's marketing messages are surrounded with clean, empty space, an effect that is remarkable in the crowded urban landscape. Only one or two images are used with each message, and few words. Willer says this approach required the client to be brave because it runs counter to so many conventions of normally riotous Russian advertising.

"The client has been passionate about developing this brand. They really understand the need for creating a brand that cuts through the clutter," she adds.

Beeline always had fair prices, so it was respected by customers. But since the new brand began buzzing, more customers have begun to give the company their loyalty. Beeline has moved from being trusted to being loved. The new brand is meant to inspire and encourage people, to open up new horizons of thought.

Beeline now has one distinct message, not many, says Willer. Customers understand and respond to that.

Another important part of the new Beeline identity is the use of plenty of white space. That attribute alone makes the company's messaging entirely unlike its competitors'.

наслаждайся

Beeline has moved from being trusted to being loved. The new brand is meant to inspire and encourage people, to open up new horizons of thought.

Unilever
Identity Design

Wolff Olins, London, United Kingdom

Consumers around the world choose Unilever products 150 million times every day, yet most of them are unaware of it. Unilever is a blue-chip company by any standard, but as a brand it is almost invisible in most Western countries.

By the time Wolff Olins began working with Unilever, in early 2002, the decision had been made to make more of the Unilever brand. The first task was to articulate what the business stood for, something that could be an anchor and touchstone for Unilever in the future. "The idea was that Unilever adds vitality to life," explains Lee Coomber, Wolff Olins creative director for Unilever's new identity project.

"The idea of vitality gives everyone in Unilever a shared sense of purpose. It suggests a new way of thinking and behaving, and it guides the organization's crucial investment and innovation decisions. Importantly, it also drives Unilever's program for social and environmental responsibility."

Unilever's existing logo suggested a steel company rather than something that felt vital or that consumers would put on or in their body.

The design team did not feel a reductionist logo would be a good fit for such a rich and diverse company. "No other company covers everything from household cleaner to fish fingers—no one else has the breadth of product. Another thing to consider was that the company has always had strong values in terms of the environment, in terms of being beneficial," Coomber says.

The designers wanted to celebrate this by representing the three main areas—people, products, and the environment—and so created twenty-five icons, each with a tie to at least one of the three categories. For example, a fish is a symbol of food but also of the environment. A palm tree represents paradise for people in northern climates, but it represents a staple food crop to some in southern realms.

Combining these icons into one symbol, the letter U, the design team created a demonstrative logo that tells a rich story of the company. Its complexity flies in the face of most logo design theory, but the simple letterform makes it work, even when print applications are less than ideal.

The new logo, although it is based on a letterform from the alphabet—the one used to write English—still has international appeal because of its simple shape. Even better, Coomber reports that audiences around the world see different messages in it, messages that feel personal.

"Some people say it looks like a henna tattoo. Some see Delft pottery. Other people see something aboriginal. That pleased us enormously," he says.

Design Firm	Turner Duckworth
Client	Brains Brewing
Project	Identity/Packaging Redesign

The name of the largest independent brewer in Wales sounds odd to anyone outside the region: Brains. This family name has been on the business since 1882. The brewery now operates about 250 pubs, where it serves its traditional beers to very loyal customers.

In 2004, the company faced this situation: it wanted to preserve and enhance customer loyalty but absolutely had to connect with its newest employees. These employees had worked for a number of smaller regional breweries Brains had purchased, and like many people in this situation, they felt disheartened and disenfranchised.

> The old Brains logo was much like that found at other traditional British pubs.

Brains management wanted to create a positive experience for everyone, customers and employees alike. It also wanted to reflect a sense of national pride, which was on the upswing in Wales.

"Cardiff, the capital of Wales, has had a big upsurge in its fortunes," explains Bruce Duckworth of Turner Duckworth, the design firm tapped by Brains to redesign its logo and identity. "Traditionally, Cardiff had a mining culture. Today, the city is coming back to the forefront with a new opera house, a Welsh Assembly Building, and its own governmental buildings. There really is a sense of renewed national pride."

The old Brains logo was much like that found at other traditional British pubs—an almost stereotypical crest from long ago. It did, however, include a dragon, a positive and patriotic symbol also found on the Welsh flag.

"We thought the logo looked medieval, like a coat of arms," recalls Duckworth. "The dragon is the national symbol of Wales, so it is an appropriate symbol. But this one looked old. The curly chain effect underneath is particularly medieval."

The creative team decided to keep the dragon but reconsidered it in a contemporary light. How could the symbol be made more relevant for today? Dragons are all about fire and aggression, but the original dragon looked a bit passive. Even more, he was walking in the wrong direction.

Brains Brewery is a venerable company with a brand-new logo, compliments of Turner Duckworth, London and San Francisco. The new identity is decidedly traditional but has plenty of contemporary flair.

The original Brains identity was relatively innocuous. Its dragon was flat, not fierce; its typography was generic; and, after many decades, its chain element had become meaningless.

The Turner Duckworth team had to respect the original logo, but they also wanted to create a mark that customers and employees—some of whom had just been brought into the Brains fold through acquisitions—could all get behind. The dragon was a heraldic symbol, but the designers felt they could make it more modern. Turning the creature to the forward-facing position also improved the design. The chain could be deleted, but its color could be reused, as these trials show.

This comparison of the old (left) and new (right) dragons shows how much the animal was changed. The new version is prouder and more highly dimensional.

The handwritten annotations on the sketch read:

- dragon in embossed out with radised corners
- tail is a radius profile
- wings are scalloped with a curved leading edge
- back leg and back wing embossed lower than main body

Gold outer

Black background

embossed dragon (see detail)

Gold horizon
grey background

grey b'ground

Gold type outline

Gold outer

nb. Sign should also have the same 3D "button" section left to right.

curved top squared off bottom

Squared off inner section curved outer section

ESTD 1882

BRAINS

This logo had to make employees and citizens feel proud.

All heraldry symbols, like the dragon and chain, had high significance at one time. So the creative team consulted extensively with coats-of-arms experts to make sure that turning the dragon around wouldn't be a graphic faux pas. They discovered that at one time the direction the dragon faced on a knight's shield indicated whether he was right- or left-handed. But that significance was certainly no longer relevant.

The chain element, once representative of a piece of cloth around the base of a knight's helmet, also no longer had meaning. It could be deleted or reworked.

The first change the designers made was to make the dragon face and walk to the right—forward, so to speak. They also made the creature look prouder and gave it more personality, whereas the previous dragon was flatly generic.

Although the team played with modern interpretations of the chain element underneath the dragon, this was ultimately replaced with a smooth, golden horizon line that emphasized the forward motion of the creature.

"The dragon is more heroic now. He is leaning forward, striving, coming up over a golden horizon. He also has flecks and highlights of gold that add to his dimension," Duckworth says.

The client liked the design that shows the dragon coming over a golden horizon. To test the design in context, the Turner Duckworth designers applied it to various elements that would be seen in and around a pub, including signage and tap handles (right). They also drew up specs for signage that accentuated the dimensionality of the design.

The typography, too, was changed extensively. Rather than use a predictable and generic serif face, the designers created a more ownable, hand-drawn sans serif that curves in relationship with the horizon line. It is much more modern and strong, and, when used separately from the dragon, is still readily identifiable as a Brains symbol.

The entire creative team was pleased with the outcome, as were the people at Brains. "Sometimes we are asked to do a logo and are aware that we are really just freshening things up. But this logo had a lot more to do—to make employees and citizens feel proud," says Duckworth. "All the new employees in the new operation have a new logo they recognize as theirs."

Duckworth says that since the new identity has been in use, sales have increased 28 percent: "Not bad for a product that has been around for over 100 years," he adds.

The new design has enormous presence and reflects the pride of its region of origin, Cardiff, Wales. The typography is also modern and strong. It is an identity that employees are proud to claim, especially on the jerseys of professional football players.

Heavenly is a new brand with a mission: to launch products of all sorts and donate a portion of sales to nonprofit organizations. Heavenly embraces the concept of embedded giving—that is, as consumers get, they give. The company asked Turner Duckworth to create a logo for its brand that could work across many disparate products, from cafés to insurance to wine.

Heavenly was ready to launch its first product, an online wine store that sells more than 300 brands of fine wine, plus its own wine as well. The embedded giving for this product donates to Water Aid, which provides clean water for the world's poorest people. When you purchase the product, you literally can change wine to water, says Bruce Duckworth, principal of Turner Duckworth, the design office that created Heavenly's new identity.

"The most important thing was to give the name *Heavenly* a meaning that had nothing to do with heaven," laughs Duckworth in his London office. The brand was not meant to allude to anything religious, or, even worse, to sound pompous or pious. Heavenly was more of an adverb, as in being able to help other people while you are enjoying a good wine or other high-quality product. "Sounds heavenly, doesn't it?"

The Turner Duckworth designers experimented with four approaches, all meant to convey heavenly yet down-to-earth thinking and attitude, Duckworth says. The first design involved using the word *heavenly* as a suffix to just about anything:

"a good cup of tea...Heavenly"; "a great ice-cold vodka...Heavenly"; or even "hassle-free insurance... Heavenly." This concept could also be expressed in shorthand, more of a logo, as just "...h."

Another design used three little characters to deliver a familiar message: "Hear, see, and speak no evil." Heavenly was all about its straightforward method—a brand that cut through the marketing rubbish that prevents customers from understanding products. "They don't flower up their message," Duckworth says.

A third concept used a downward-pointing bracket to communicate the idea of benefit coming from heaven. The design that eventually won starts with this thought and makes it into a strong, singular logo featuring a lowercase h with a five-pointed star beneath it. The negative space between these two elements creates a downward-pointing arrow, bringing heaven down to Earth. This formed a logo that was both ownable and meaningful for the client.

Heavenly, still a fledgling company, is using its new identity on its first brand, heavenly wine (www.heavenlywine.co.uk). The logo works well, Duckworth says, because it represents the attitude of the company in a distinctive and simple way rather than relating to a particular product. Heavenly can go into many diverse areas and still use the same logo, because its ethos of embedded giving will always be relevant.

...heavenly

HEAVENLY
DOWN TO EARTH CONSULTANCY ™

heavenly™

marketing

heavenlyvodka
★

ice cold
pure russian
vodka...
heavenly
★

Design Firm	Werner Design Werks
Client	Moët Hennessy
Project	Identity/Packaging Design

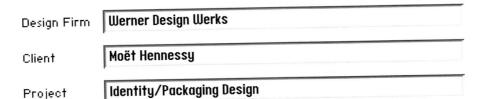

10 Cane is a high-end, light amber-colored clear rum made from the first press of a new sugarcane crop. It is a liquor made for mixing with fresh juices, fruit, other liquor—or, of course, Coke. But it is not meant for every-day drinks; it might be purchased for home consumption, but 10 Cane is much more likely to be enjoyed mixed into a $10 cocktail at a trendy club, says Sharon Werner of Werner Design Werks, Minneapolis. Her firm was hired by distiller Moët Hennessy to name and create an identity for the then-unnamed rum in 2003.

"It's a rum for people who want the best rum and Coke they have ever had, the kind of cocktail that Ernest Hemingway would have ordered, the classic cocktail," says Werner.

> **10 Cane is a rum for people who want the best rum and Coke they have ever had.**

The fact that the rum can be produced only when the new cane crop is ready automatically makes it an expensive product, about $40 per liter. Its exotic, exclusive origin and traditional brewing process make it unique, almost alchemic.

"The client wanted to play into the mixology and alchemy of a cocktail. This rum fit because it is made in a very old way but produced as a contemporary luxury brand. The alchemy was there, so the identity had to have the same feel," Werner says.

Prior to Werner Design's work on the project, Moët Hennessy had worked with Fallon Brand Consulting to determine the feasibility of the brand. Fallon spent a year determining who would buy the rum and how they would drink it. The firm's findings ran counter to the notion of a "spring break rum," which might be consumed not only in great quantity but also in fruity, sugary drinks.

This new brand was far more restrained. It had to feel modern enough to mix in easily at the club scene but also look as if it had been around for a long time, Werner says. "Our target customer was a twenty-three- to thirty-five-year-old male you might see at the airport with a beat-up but highest-quality briefcase. He has comfortable but high-quality clothing, a vintage Rolex, and an iPod. He is comfortable with traveling and flying. He probably has everything he needs for two weeks in a small carry-on. The brand had to be like that—not trying overly hard to impress."

10 Cane is a high-end rum, meant to stand out in an elegant way in trendy clubs. Werner Design Werks created its identity and packaging, an alchemic mix of old and new.

To communicate that 10 Cane is a new product made using an age-old recipe, designers Sharon Werner and Sarah Nelson at first considered a flask bottle design. This idea was eventually discarded because of production concerns, but the design of the crest-like logo combined with a modern paper label was retained.

(Above) This sloped-shoulder bottle is plain but classic. Its long neck, covered with texture, makes it stand out on the crowded bar shelf and is easy for bartenders to grip.

(Left) Imprinting a heraldic crest on the bottle gave it an aged look. Elements include monkeys, foliage, sugarcane, and engraved currency. But the addition of the warm orange paper label—various trials are shown here—gives the design contemporary confidence.

The new name not only refers to the main ingredient but also has the sense of an age-old recipe.

Werner and Nelson also experimented with color combinations. The key was to make the viewer understand immediately that this was rum, not vodka or any other clear liquor.

The name of the product (determined with the help of copywriter Jeff Mueller) came from the rum's recipe: it takes ten canes of sugar cane to produce one bottle of the product. It was a name that didn't feel fussy, a name the target buyer could say comfortably when ordering.

"Moët Hennessy is in Paris, and they really depended on us to reach the U.S. market correctly. The client wanted a name and design that clearly separated the product from vodka or any other clear liquor. We had to create a new language," recalls Werner. The new name not only refers to the main ingredient but also has the sense of an age-old recipe.

Werner and designer Sarah Nelson started their explorations of the bottle design by considering where it would live. To be successful in a club, a bottle must be bartender-friendly. Bartenders must be happy with how a bottle feels and performs. It can't slip out of their hands, and they want to look good while pouring from it. Plenty of testing occurred at this stage, all aimed at determining exact user preferences.

The cocktail buyer wants the bartender to look good, too. "For a $10 cocktail, it is as much about enjoying the mixing performance as it is about the taste of the finished drink," Werner notes.

With clearance from the client to design a custom bottle, Werner and Nelson considered carefully how its shape could become a vital part of the new identity. One design they particularly liked resembled an old flask with an offset neck, but the bottle manufacturer was unable to produce it in quantity.

Even though this shape felt good to the hand and the focus group liked it too, Werner says that in the end, she was glad the design didn't make it to the shelves. It was too trendy and therefore would not have had staying power.

"By the end of two years, everyone would have been tired of it. The bottle we decided on is simple and plain but appropriate and classic," she says.

The finished bottle has rounded shoulders and a long neck that is easy to hold, with little grippers. The base is of comfortable gripping width as well.

The bottle has aspects of modern and old, as does the product's logo. To design the mark, the designers studied heraldry as well as the history of Trinidad and the Caribbean, places that had a long history with rum. Sketching went on for several months as they mixed images of monkeys, sugarcane, currency—like seals, and many other engraved elements. They worked in a nondigital way, Werner recalls, drawing, redrawing, and combining tissues.

As they developed what is essentially a crest, flowing vegetation was added to suggest that the rum is a natural product. Crossed sugarcanes form an X to indicate the number of canes used for each bottle. A castle turret was inspired by the architecture of Trinidad and even France.

"The helmet? We don't really have a great reason for it. It just felt good. The important thing was to not get too highbrow with any one part," Werner says.

The final art, rendered by Elvis Swift, looks as though it may have been branded into wooden crates for hundreds of years. It is applied directly to the bottle. The contemporary touch comes from a warm, glossy orange paper label carrying the product name. The label is applied directly on top of the crest for a real contrast between old and new.

Werner says the design stands out in the club atmosphere, surrounded as it is with brands designed to be temporary. It is a classic look, meant to inspire the loyalty of drinkers who are comfortable with themselves. It is not intended to attract the trendy.

"The design catches customers' eyes, and the quality of the product sustains product loyalty," Werner says. The mix of contemporary design and traditional distilling is a strangely effective alchemy that is carried into the product's advertising. One ad shows a man in a tuxedo standing in a field of sugarcane—it's a strange but intriguing juxtaposition.

"It's a mix of old and new, of high and low. Together, the identity and the product look cool and right together," the designer says.

Here the designers screenprinted on both sides of the embossed bottle, creating many levels of interest. The type and crest are printed in two layers, orange directly under black. In this way, the orange shows through on one side, but the same image appears in black when the bottle is rotated.

(Above) More design trials combining paper labels, color, and printing.

(Left) As the new identity is played out in advertising and promotion, the same orange color and label are used—a clear identifier for the brand.

Cameo
Identity Design

Werner Design Werks, Minneapolis, Minnesota

Cameo is curious combination of beauty salon and social club. In fact, designer Sarah Nelson of Werner Design Werks calls it a "beauty lounge." Located near several trendy Minneapolis restaurants, Cameo is a place to see and be seen. The shop sells cosmetics and baubles, and it has a comfortable lounge area where the thirty- to forty-year-old set can gather to mingle, shop, get a manicure, and even enjoy a few drinks.

"The businesswomen who founded Cameo are sassy and smart," says Nelson. "They are very much people who would like to have their nails done and enjoy a martini at the same time. They offer lines of care products not available elsewhere. Their salon has definitely become a destination."

Nelson and partner Sharon Werner wanted to design a logo for Cameo that had the same sassy, irrepressible attitude as the establishment. The clients wanted something sexy and provocative but not sleazy—more like fan-dancing than striptease.

The designers came up with a number of directions that had appeal. The image of a powder puff had the right combination of beauty, attention to self, and pampering. (It actually ended up being used as a secondary application in the final identity; see secondary samples.) A Kewpie doll, frilly type, birds, butterflies, baby angels, and cupids were also considered.

But the idea the designers liked best showed the figure of a woman seated inside of an illuminated letter.

"The shape of the C suited the shape of the woman's back really well," says Nelson. The figure's hair flows around the letter almost like additional flourishes. Her black-clad legs kick out in a flirty way, and she winks playfully at the viewer. She is decidedly the prominent figure in the logo, but the letter still reads well.

To keep the woman somewhat chaste, Nelson had to do a lot of drawing and redrawing to expose just the right amount of breast. The emphasis had to be on beauty and sass, not overt sexiness.

The designers and the client were pleased with the finished logo. It's fun, yet definitely provocative. "Cameo is all about saying it is OK to look at yourself in the mirror and there's nothing wrong with playing with cosmetics. I think the logo expresses that," Nelson says.

Cameo

BEAUTY LOUNGE

Cameo

BEAUTY LOUNGE

Design Firm	Carbone Smolan
Client	Fortis
Project	Logo/Identity Design

The insurance market is a saturated one. Competitors and claims of all sorts of service abound. A risk-management company with a lesser-known name than Aetna or State Farm has to work hard to gain the customer's attention and explain what makes it special.

When Fortis, an international, integrated financial services provider, decided to offer its North American insurance operations as an initial public offering (IPO) on the New York Stock Exchange, the management team of the newly independent group had to create a whole new identity within months. The new company, named Assurant, required a system that would help its businesses—Assurant Solutions, Assurant Preneed, Assurant Health, and Assurant Employee Benefits—communicate their market focus and reinforce the coherence of the group. Finally, the identity had to say a lot about how Assurant's integrated offerings would benefit customers.

ASSURANT

> The challenge was to develop an identity that emphasized the coherence of the new group as well as its specialized niche services.

Assurant's new logo and identity is bright, lively, and meaningful: It symbolizes the united energies of all lines of the company's subsidiaries.

Landor Associates designed the original Fortis logo. Its design was meant to suggest the idea of Fortis being part of the communities where it had businesses. Carbone Smolan Agency, the design firm selected by Assurant to create the new identity, was asked to leverage the logo's bright, lively color system and visuals. The challenge was to develop an identity that emphasized the coherence of the new group as well as its specialized niche services.

FORTIS

The logo for Fortis, Assurant's previous identity, designed by Landor Associates, was meant to suggest that Fortis was an integral part of the communities in which it operates.

"Assurant integrates a trio of strengths: risk management expertise, administrative systems, and distribution relationships. It offers technical solutions to other companies and insurance to young people who are just coming off of their parents' insurance. It offers employee benefits to small- to mid-sized companies as well as preneed insurance—that is, insurance for funeral expenses," explains Catherine Goodman, Carbone Smolan project director. "We needed to somehow gather all of these strengths of the different businesses and communicate one strong company."

The Carbone Smolan team devised five distinct concepts for the client. The first had a connections focus. It demonstrated how the client connected with its customers, providing coverage for niche areas as well as

Carbone Smolan's woven graphic solution pulls together the core elements of the company. It can be displayed in a horizontal orientation with the wordmark, or the graphic can be run above the name (see introduction to article). The typeface Geometric was altered to mimic the rounded triangular shapes inside of the logo.

We needed to somehow gather all of these strengths of the different businesses and communicate one strong company.

excellent protection. This approach included graphics that showed bridges connecting land masses.

A second concept also looked at connections and bridges, but it was much more abstract. The designs in this group focused more on the wordmark.

One idea the designers liked was focusing graphically on the three capabilities the company offers. "We wanted to show that Assurant is specialized, focused, and integrated," says Dominick Ricci, Carbone Smolan designer for the project. This idea actually was the starting point for the final design solution, which came to be known as the "weave symbol."

> The idea was to show complex ideas such as aerodynamics through greatly simplified visual concepts.

To demonstrate the client's ability to handle complex concepts and situations clearly and competently, the design team also developed a tapestry concept. The weave in this design came from the letterforms themselves being woven together. "This showed that the company was complex. But the integration of the parts created a greater whole," explains Ricci.

The idea of growth emerged in the next set of designs. Here, the designers wanted to show Assurant's ability to form broad networks and achieve superior results for policyholders. These designs borrowed from images in nature to suggest growth.

Balance was the centerpiece of yet another set of designs. "The tightrope walkers were meant to show how Assurant brings balance to relationships," says Ricci. "The triangle forms a strong base that other things can rest safely on."

The penultimate design ended up the favorite. It demonstrated partnership. "These designs were all based around the ampersand," says Ricci.

But the idea that eventually emerged as the winner was a woven graphic that pulled together the core elements of the company. The final logo integrates the three niche offerings in a way that shows solid strength. A complete unit is formed, but the original three strengths are still distinct. Tucked inside is the suggestion of the letter A as well as a distinctly broad-based and stable triangle. (The idea for the A came from an Assurant executive with a keen interest in architecture.) To reinforce the shape, the designers modified the typeface Geometric for the wordmark to mimic the rounded triangle shape inside the mark.

"The typeface is very solid—it inspires confidence," says Ricci. "We ran it in a warm gray for even more strength and to play off the livelier colors we chose for the logo."

The other three colors—a blue, a green, and an orange—were favorites with the client almost from the beginning of the project. The traditional blue was Assurant's one remaining visual tie to the Fortis identity; the vibrant green and bright orange play well against it.

In advertising, the identity's vibrant color scheme is played out even further through metaphorical art—another way for the designers to explain in simple terms the client's complex product offerings.

The new color scheme became a crucial part of how the identity was introduced to the public. In ads that appeared in the *New York Times, Wall Street Journal,* and hundreds of other business and regional publications, the colors were played out through visual metaphors—a blue, green, and orange kite to demonstrate aerodynamics, and a similarly colored yo-yo to suggest gravity.

"The whole idea was to show complex ideas such as aerodynamics through greatly simplified visual concepts. The ads really stood out in the different publications," says Ricci. It is a value-added concept: Assurant specializes so it can make something as complicated as insurance simple for its customers.

Ricci and Goodman felt the final solution was fresh yet serious, appropriate for a company of Assurant's stature. "Boiling something as complex as a diversified insurance company down to something so simple and clear is very satisfying. There is a real story behind this logo; we really know what each stroke and color is about," Ricci says.

The new mark can be run in full color or no color, in large sizes or small, and still reads well.

The final logo integrates the three niche offerings in a way that shows solid strength.

Brooklyn Botanic Garden
Identity Design

Carbone Smolan, New York, New York

More than 100 years old in the making, Brooklyn Botanic Garden (BBG) was a living gem hidden just minutes from Manhattan. But beyond its immediate neighborhood, it was largely an unknown resource.

"People outside of the area did not realize what a great place it is," says Elizabeth Amorose, project director at Carbone Smolan Agency (CSA), the design firm that undertook a rebranding of the garden to correct this problem.

The garden's management is in the process of instituting plenty of facilities improvements, and it was clear a rebranding was necessary to raise the garden's status from a local attraction to a world-class institution. The Art Deco-like logo had been in use since the 1970s. The in-house team wanted something much more modern in feel.

"We did a lot of upfront strategizing with the client," says Carla Miller, design director at CSA. "We pared it down to several key words: *modern, growth,* and *plant life.* But no one wanted a literal drawing of a plant. They wanted a symbol."

After creating trial designs—including an abstract rendering of the Tree of Heaven (also known as the Chinese sumac); a tree described in the book *A Tree Grows in Brooklyn;* an abstract, rotating flower shape that evoked *change* and *beauty;* and an avant-garde monogram of BBG (eliminated because the garden couldn't go with a purely initial-based name)—CSA designers developed a mark that clearly demonstrated budding growth. Spare yet formal, the mark intertwines the three major focuses of the garden: research and education (represented by blue), people and events (orange), and plant life (green).

"The mark represents plant life without being any particular plant," explains Amorose.

Another vital part of the identity is a long, arching line, actually one of the spires in the logo played out at a much greater scale. Based on the Fibonacci series, the equation that underlies the shape of all organic life, the blade is used as a container for imagery and text on the garden's website and across all of its materials—brochures, banners, and so on.

The complete identity is endlessly flexible. Interplayed with any number of floral and greenery elements from the garden, depending on the season and on events in the garden, it stays fresh and interesting.

Miller feels the mark and blade work well together to build a strong brand platform. "It's much more than just a logo. The new tagline, 'Where Plants Come to Life', which we also developed, is another important part," she explains.

Few large gardens do a good job of promoting themselves, so it was easy to make BBG stand out. "If the client wants to be known as a world-class facility, its identity cannot look home-grown," says Amorose. "BBG had the reputation of being more of a mom-and-pop operation. Now it is known as a world-class cultural institution."

Design Firm	Michael Osborne Design
Client	Target / Archer Farms
Project	Logo and Packaging Design

Target Corporation has become well known for offering its customers smart pricing and good design. Over the past decade, this value-added concept has been carried out across every category of product its stores carry.

At Target and Super Target stores, which include a full-service grocery, the company carries its own line of foods in addition to national brands. The Target brand, called Archer Farms, was meant to be an upscale line with a premium look. It sits on the shelves with a second Target brand that is the store's more price-conscious line. Archer Farms offerings were a bit more exotic; instead of just hot or mild salsa, for instance, it let the consumer choose between peach mango and three-bean varieties.

The new logo and identity design had to look clearly more upscale than the price-conscious line.

The trouble was that a recent redesign of the price-conscious line made it look quite clean and attractive. In fact, it suddenly looked better than the Archer Farms brand. The upscale brand needed a new look, too. Target asked Michael Osborne Design, San Francisco—a design firm known for its classic but modern look—to undertake the identity makeover.

"Previously, the entire Archer Farms brand was color-coded in greens," explains principal Michael Osborne. "Whenever you saw the color green, you knew it was the private-label Target brand."

This simple approach was no longer effective. The new logo and identity design had to look clearly more upscale than the price-conscious line. It had to be consistently applicable to a wide variety of products, from popcorn to pasta and from bottled water to bottled sauces. Finally, it had to compete smartly with upscale national and regional brands.

These are relatively broad design directives, and the design team could have gone in many directions. Osborne's approach was to imagine the project objectives as a three-dimensional sphere. "When we are creating such a holistic system, we try to throw design darts and hit the sphere, but from all different directions, from different points of view. All the darts hit the target and accomplish the design goals, but in different ways," he explains.

His team presented a number of concepts. One direction featured round shapes and bright colors—"upscale, but more happy in a Target kind of

(Above) Archer Farms, Target Corporation's premium food line, now has a distinctive, upscale look, thanks to Michael Osborne Design.

(Right) When a more price-conscious Target food line was redesigned, the previous Archer Farms line, set entirely in green, no longer had the upscale look it needed to distinguish itself.

(Below) The Michael Osborne Design team explored a number of directions. These trials had a natural, earthy feel. They used kraft paper and unpretentious ties, combined with simple typography and colors, to create an Old-World-meets-modern-Target look.

(Above) These explorations were more in keeping with the storewide Target identity: bouncy, geometric, bright. Colors and typography were also vibrant and modern.

It is just as important to cover the full array of ideas, even the extreme ones, so the client is exposed to the full range of creative possibilities.

way," explains Osborne. Highly geometric, this design approach complemented the Target logo with its primary color palette and shapes.

Another suggested design direction had a natural, earthy feeling. It used natural kraft paper and bags for packaging, interesting and unusual structures and closures, and the branding and typography had an Old-World-Italy-meets-modern-Target look.

A third concept looked simply gorgeous and gourmet, says Osborne, like the packaging that might be found on a line of foods in a specialty market. It featured luscious photography, a rich color palette, and elegant typography. It was perhaps too upscale, he adds, but it is just as important to cover the full array of ideas—even the extreme ones—so the client is exposed to the full range of creative possibilities.

Osborne stands behind all directions that are presented in these types of projects. He often makes recommendations based on what his team feels will compete most effectively in the marketplace. In this case, Target agreed that a "French country-with-a-modern-twist" concept worked best. At its center was a simple brand identity: a rooster, sitting proudly inside a low-slung oval, together with the motto "Tasty Food, Tasty Price." This mark sat easily on all types of packaging: bags, cans, bottle, jars. Combined with a palette of rich reds, greens, blues, yellows, and black, the logo stands out as a ready identifier on shelves populated with obnoxiously colored packaging.

Aesthetics aside, the identity worked well for every sort of printing the Archer Farms packaging required. Its simplicity allowed it to be stamped onto plastic bags as successfully and cleanly as it could be four-color offset-printed on paper.

Some products utilized beautiful, up-close color photographs set off by a dark hunter-green background with a diamond pattern. Other products featured clear structures or unusual substrates, such as a metallic silver-foil coffee bag.

Osborne feels one reason the design is successful is because it is so different from the standard Target branding and the red bull's-eye, yet it works well in context and complements the other offerings to the Target consumer.

"It's an upscale food line. When you pick up a product, it really does look delicious, while being reasonably priced," he says. "'Expect more, pay less', the Target motto, has never been truer."

(Above) The final identity looks decidedly gourmet. It has a rich color scheme, upscale typography, and a sense of history.

(Opposite) Applied to packaging, the new logo and identity cuts through the jumble of color and graphics on the Target shelves. It is so simple that it prints well on any substrate and through any printing method.

Hearts in San Francisco
Identity Design

Michael Osborne Design, San Francisco, California

Hearts in San Francisco was an initiative by private citizens to raise money for the San Francisco General Hospital Foundation. It was modeled on efforts made in other cities across the country in which a geographically apt icon is dressed by many local artists. In Chicago, cows were appropriate. In San Francisco, it had to be hearts.

Michael Osborne Design was asked by the Hearts steering committee to create the two crucial portions of the effort's identity: First, he designed a pair of large, three-dimensional hearts. Artists could pick one of the two to paint or otherwise alter to express their message. Once all 130 sculptures were done, they were displayed throughout the city as public art installations. These formed the public face of the program.

The two hearts had different personalities. "The first thing I thought of was a big, round, full heart with its point on the ground—a big, voluptuous heart. I wanted a different form for the second one. I actually based it on a sculpture I did in seventh-grade shop class. It has big, intersecting plates," the designer says.

Osborne also created a logo for the program, to be used on collateral, the group's website (www.heartsinsf.com), advertising, and on banners and other signage. It was important that the logo not compete with the artists' sculptures for attention. The design had to be in line with traditional corporate identity, yet be more expressive.

His solution, created after about 100 trials with a paintbrush (all untouched by Photoshop, he says), is clearly related to the arts, but its solid typography grounds it in a formal way. "It needed flair, spontaneity, and energy, but it does not compete with the artists," Osborne says.

At the end of the exhibition, a live auction was held to sell the twenty-five hearts that had special meaning to the city or were created by the most prominent artists. The remainder were auctioned off on eBay. The proceeds, combined with the sales of a keepsake book that displayed all of the hearts, raised just over $2 million for the Foundation.

Osborne says that although the project was meant to be a one-time event, the organizers have received many requests to do it again.

collections and sketches

	A	B	C	D

1   **LOGO SEARCH**

Keywords [Initials]

Type: ○ Symbol   ○ Typographic   ○ Combo   ● All

2

 AFTER5 COMPANIES

A·E·T·H·E·R

3

  AIRLUME CANDLES

ALLSCRIPTS

4

  AGENDAONE

AIAS

5

 A TO Z MEDIA

⊡ = Design Firm   ⊙ = Client

1C ⊡ Chimera Design ⊙ Victorian Aquatic Industry Council   1D ⊡ traci jones design ⊙ Creative Alliance

2A ⊡ Rule 29 ⊙ After 5   2B ⊡ Doink, Inc. ⊙ Avanti Men's Store   2C ⊡ dandy idea ⊙ Alexis and Brian Ferguson   2D ⊡ Werner Design Werks ⊙ Aether for Nike

3A ⊡ Fauxkoi ⊙ FauxKoi Design   3B ⊡ Roger Christian & Co ⊙ Airlume Candles   3C ⊡ Steven O'Connor ⊙ Allscripts   3D ⊡ Lesniewicz Associates ⊙ Jamiesons Audio/Video

4A ⊡ Pixelube ⊙ Artocracy   4B ⊡ The Meyocks Group ⊙ Agenda One   4C ⊡ Archrival ⊙ American Institute of Architecture Students   4D ⊡ Ikola designs... ⊙ The Associated Architects

5A ⊡ Dotzero Design ⊙ Alternate Universe Events   5B ⊡ Jason Kirshenblatt ⊙ A to Z Media   5C ⊡ Leeann Leftwich Zajas Design ⊙ The Boston Conservatory   5D ⊡ Strategy Studio ⊙ Barton's Chocolates

	A	B	C	D	

1

2

3

4

5

Ⓓ = Design Firm   Ⓒ = Client

1A Ⓓ Paul Black Design Ⓒ Burns Service Company   1B Ⓓ Henjum Creative Ⓒ Badger Paper Mills   1C Ⓓ Ikola designs... Ⓒ Brunswick United Methodist Church   1D Ⓓ Landkamer Partners, Inc. Ⓒ Biogenics

2A Ⓓ Steven O'Connor Ⓒ B 10   2B Ⓓ Ross Hogin Design Ⓒ Boticelli Pastaworks   2C Ⓓ Ikola designs... Ⓒ burningham Weavers   2D Ⓓ Mindgruve Ⓒ Blue Motif

3A Ⓓ Whaley Design, Ltd Ⓒ Chargo Printing, Inc.   3B Ⓓ MINE Ⓒ Blaney Kravitz/Comira   3C Ⓓ GRAF d'SIGN creative boutique Ⓒ Cybico   3D Ⓓ Mariqua Design Ⓒ Clone

4A Ⓓ AKOFA Creative Ⓒ Self Promotional   4B Ⓓ Werner Design Werks Ⓒ Chandler Atwood   4C Ⓓ R&D Thinktank Ⓒ Capital Plan   4D Ⓓ Gardner Design Ⓒ Corry Dance Academy

5A Ⓓ Jonathan Rice & Company Ⓒ Champion Energy   5B Ⓓ angryporcupine*design Ⓒ Cheryl Dailey   5C Ⓓ Werner Design Werks Ⓒ College of Visual Arts   5D Ⓓ Duffy & Partners Ⓒ Duffy & Partners

71

	A	B	C	D
1				
2				
3				
4				
5				

	A	B	C	D

    1

    2

    3

    4

5

Ⓓ = Design Firm   Ⓒ = Client

1A Ⓓ Dotzero Design Ⓒ Ecos   1B Ⓓ Peterson & Company Ⓒ Engenium   1C Ⓓ Brand Bird Ⓒ emerald Graphics   1D Ⓓ FutureBrand Ⓒ Millicom Argentina

2A Ⓓ ODM oficina de diseño y marketing Ⓒ Eléctrica Bahia   2B Ⓓ Diagram Ⓒ E24 Internet Club   2C Ⓓ marc usa Ⓒ Fleck Photography   2D Ⓓ Duffy & Partners Ⓒ Thymes

3A Ⓓ McMillian Design Ⓒ Fulton Street BID   3B Ⓓ Mode Design Studio Ⓒ Folinger Mountainwear   3C Ⓓ designlab, inc Ⓒ Weissman's Dance   3D Ⓓ IMAGEHAUS Ⓒ Far Fetched Spirits

4A Ⓓ Interrobang Design Collaborative, Inc. Ⓒ FM Group Public Relations   4B Ⓓ Tactical Magic Ⓒ The Eyewear Gallery   4C Ⓓ Allen Creative Ⓒ Grace Fellowship   4D Ⓓ ComGroup Ⓒ ComGroup

5A Ⓓ Diagram Ⓒ Kulczyk Foundation   5B Ⓓ GetElevatedDesign.com Ⓒ Green Lotus Grounds   5C Ⓓ Crackerbox Ⓒ G.W.Engineering   5D Ⓓ Diagram Ⓒ Horyzon Publishing

	A	B	C	D
1				
2				
3				
4				
5				

D = Design Firm   C = Client

1A D Diagram C Horse Publishing   1B D Gardner Design C Hustler   1C D Ross Hogin Design C HRCentral   1D D Deep Design C The Henritze Company, LLC

2A D Zed+Zed+Eye Creative Communications C Hilliards Insulation   2B D Dialekt Design C Timex (JDK)   2C D Gardner Design C Hustler   2D D Sibley Peteet C Horizon Printing

3A D Sibley Peteet C Ryan and Dinah Street   3B D Q C Hessen Chemie   3C D Ikola designs... C Ikola designs...   3D D Ardoise Design C Immotik inc.

4A D Bryan Cooper Design C Impact Productions   4B D Sockeye Creative C ieLogic   4C D Eisenberg and Associates C IT Rescue   4D D Kendall Creative Shop, Inc. C Jarvis Press

5A D B.L.A. Design Company C Nathan Good   5B D DDB Dallas C Kemp Academy of Tae Kwon Do and Hapkido   5C D Lesniewicz Associates C Kuhlman Corp.   5D D Funk/Levis & Associates, Inc. C Kelly King & Associates

kea Quality Print

KONTRAPUNKT

PREMIUM
LUSOMUNDO

1

Landes Investments

lenox graphics

MERCURY

2

mobimax

 Metro

3

MUTTMINSTER

M

THE IOWA
MUTT SHOW

ANIMAL RESCUE LEAGUE OF IOWA

McMillen

4

MicroInteractive

merchant**logix**

MetroNational
BANK & TRUST

5

	A	B	C	D
1	 MetroWest		NUANCE	
2		Netscape	napa valley vintners	Notiva
3	NouvelleVie Opaque	NUANCE AV	orthomol	oretum
4	THE OCEAN CLUB		OTTER CREEK MALL	
5	PIVOT180™			

1

2

3

4

5

A　　　B　　　C　　　D

Ⓓ = Design Firm　　Ⓒ = Client

1A Ⓓ R&D Thinktank Ⓒ Quady Painting 1B Ⓓ KOESTER design Ⓒ Q ink 1C Ⓓ ROAD design inc. Ⓒ Pairgain 1D Ⓓ Fernandez Design Ⓒ TorchQuest

2A Ⓓ Jon Flaming Design Ⓒ Proposed Quark Logo 2B Ⓓ UlrichPinciotti Design Group Ⓒ Quantum Group 2C Ⓓ Wilkinson Media Ⓒ I-Quotient 2D Ⓓ Axiom Design Partners Ⓒ Quality Press

3A Ⓓ Allen Creative Ⓒ River Rehab 3B Ⓓ octane inc. Ⓒ Rustad Marketing 3C Ⓓ Edward Allen Ⓒ Revolve Motion 3D Ⓓ Gardner Design Ⓒ Relianz Bank

4A Ⓓ The Meyocks Group Ⓒ rubberdisc.com 4B Ⓓ rajasandhu.com Ⓒ First Rate 4C Ⓓ Rick Johnson & Company Ⓒ Rick Johnson & Company 4D Ⓓ Gardner Design Ⓒ Russell Public Relations

5A Ⓓ Gardner Design Ⓒ Relianz Bank 5B Ⓓ Henjum Creative Ⓒ Oshkosh Symphony Orchestra 5C Ⓓ Moscato Design Ⓒ Simpson's 5D Ⓓ Strategy Studio Ⓒ Strategy Studio

	A	B	C	D

A   **B**   **C**   **D**

1

2

3

4

5

A	B	C	D	
				1
				2
				3
				4
				5

	A	B	C	D
1				
2				
3			eighth floor recording studio	elevenfeetmedia
4	SIXTEEN		41Seventy STUDIO	
5		SEVENTOELEVEN		ReUnion 2001

M5 Coke
Identity Design

mk12, Kansas City, Missouri

How do you turn a consumer product into an event? That's what the Coca-Cola Company asked the design office mk12, as well as four other offices around the world. The answer: Take two of the most common design icons found anywhere—the Coke logo and the Coke bottle—and transform them into something that defies expectations.

A core creative team at Coke contacted five teams known for their thought-provoking graphics and motion graphics work: mk12 (Kansas City, MO/North America); REX and Tennant McKay (South Africa); Lobo (Brazil); The Designers Republic (United Kingdom); and Caviar (Japan). The client's instructions were minimal: Each team should create a new Coke identity using a metal bottle and building off of the word *optimism.* Each team was also asked to produce a music video bringing its design to life through motion and sound.

Ben Radatz, partner at mk12, explains that Coke is not trying to build its brand through the project. In fact, the five designs will be distributed only to a select group of clubs frequented by people in tune with the arts.

"Coke is more than a brand—the words *soft drink* and *Coke* are almost synonymous. Traditional branding through advertising doesn't hurt anything, but it really doesn't help the company much anymore. Everyone knows what the bottle and logo look like already," Radatz says. "With this project, Coke wants to promote the arts, in an altruistic way, as it did before with Keith Haring and Andy Warhol. The company is helping people reconsider everything."

For their design, Radatz says his team wanted to build on the way that the product's logo complements the bottle shape. The result was a complicated series of swirls, graphic flowers, silhouetted shapes, and flat colors that wrap the entire aluminum bottle and are completely unlike traditional Coke graphics. Every element can be easily animated.

Each design also has a hidden element: when placed under black light, such as might be used in a club, a hidden, secondary design is revealed. This multilevel scheme adds to the exploration and discovery aspects of what Coke calls the M5 project.

"The designs blow people's minds. They are used to a certain type of branding, and this is a complete 180 for them," Radatz says. "Converse and Volkswagen have also done experimental design like this. It could be an interesting trend in corporate design."

It was fascinating at the project's end, he adds, to discover that all the firms took the same approach—building on the swirl—as mk12, although none had consulted with the others. It's a revealing insight into the power of the Coke logo worldwide.

See all five bottle designs at www.them5.com, including the music video mk12 produced with the group Guided by Voices.

	A	B	C	D

1

LOGO SEARCH

Keywords | **Typography**

Type: ○ Symbol ○ Typographic ○ Combo ● All

blo

(poetry center san josé)

2

s☺ript:

inko

edge

Third point

3

w!se
working in support of education

karen hill scott

entertrainingEtc
educational technologies and consulting

.planum:

4

oyuna

Explore

Velotools

tifréttir

5

seas

urture CARE

OBSERVA

JASON
AND THE ARGONAUTS

ⓓ = Design Firm   ⓒ = Client

1C ⓓ Flaxenfield, Inc. ⓒ Blo, Inc. 1D ⓓ joemiller's company ⓒ Poetry Center San José

2A ⓓ McGuire Design ⓒ Script Magazine 2B ⓓ Kym Abrams Design ⓒ Ink, inc. 2C ⓓ MEME ENGINE ⓒ OMD 2D ⓓ IMA Design, Corp. ⓒ Direct mail Agency Third Point

3A ⓓ Iperdesign, Inc. ⓒ Wise 3B ⓓ Special Modern Design ⓒ dr.karen hill scott co 3C ⓓ ODM oficina de diseño y marketing ⓒ Entertraining 3D ⓓ GRAF d'Sign creative boutique ⓒ Planum

4A ⓓ Thomas Manss & Company ⓒ Oyuna Cashmere 4B ⓓ Dotfive ⓒ the Luce Foundation-Smithsonian Institute 4C ⓓ The Clockwork Group ⓒ Velotools 4D ⓓ Ó! ⓒ FÍT, Association of Icelandic Graphic Designers

5A ⓓ Kineto ⓒ Hilton Cebu Phillipines 5B ⓓ www.iseedots.com ⓒ Tungsten Design 5C ⓓ ODM oficina de diseño y marketing ⓒ Observa 5D ⓓ thielen Designs ⓒ Jason Daniello

Ⓓ = Design Firm   Ⓒ = Client

1A Ⓓ Jejak, rumah iklan dan disain Ⓒ Zone   1B Ⓓ Rotor Design Ⓒ Rotor Design   1C Ⓓ dandy idea Ⓒ Texas Commission on the Arts   1D Ⓓ Future Brand Ⓒ Wines of Chile

2A Ⓓ Bakken Creative Co. Ⓒ Frascati Restaurant   2B Ⓓ GSCS Ⓒ Bridge Business partners   2C Ⓓ Orange Creative Ⓒ Morgan Hair   2D Ⓓ Werner Design Werks Ⓒ Indochine

3A Ⓓ dedstudios Ⓒ Wildflower Linen   3B Ⓓ Times Infinity Ⓒ Home & Habitat   3C Ⓓ Judson design associates Ⓒ Lumina   3D Ⓓ NeoGine Communication Design Ltd Ⓒ Stephanie Pietkiewicz

4A Ⓓ Tiffany Design Ⓒ Classico Wine   4B Ⓓ The Design Poole Ⓒ The Military Shop   4C Ⓓ Brand Navigation Ⓒ Island Lodge   4D Ⓓ Felixsockwell.com Ⓒ nyc2012

5A Ⓓ Fredrik Lewander Ⓒ Dobb Production   5B Ⓓ dialect Design Ⓒ Toboggan Design   5C Ⓓ jsDesignCo. Ⓒ Throttle, LTD.   5D Ⓓ CAPSULE Ⓒ Lumens

83

	A	B	C	D
1	**Da:Da:Da.**	white ^{coloured by you}	clearw˙re	spa orange
2	the great lakes center for **autism**	Warm Springs REHABILITATION SYSTEM	H!gh F!ve	brilliant corporation
3	goodies	corkscrew	9below	mark. garrison
4	cutcost.com	Institute for Emerging Issues	twistology	bepositive
5	stepxstep	micropelt	loglogic	(>erb)

Ⓓ = Design Firm   Ⓒ = Client

1A Ⓓ ZEBRA design branding Ⓒ Da Da Da   1B Ⓓ Brandia Ⓒ White   1C Ⓓ Hornall Anderson Ⓒ Clearwire   1D Ⓓ Hirshorn Zuckerman Design Group Ⓒ Spa Orange

2A Ⓓ UlrichPinciotti Design Group Ⓒ Great Lakes Center for Autism   2B Ⓓ Roger Christian & Co Ⓒ Warm Springs Rehabilitation System   2C Ⓓ Peters Design Ⓒ High Five   2D Ⓓ logobyte Ⓒ Brilliant Health Corporation

3A Ⓓ Stand Advertising Ⓒ Rich Products   3B Ⓓ A3 Design Ⓒ Corkscrew Wine Bar   3C Ⓓ Brainding Ⓒ 9 Below   3D Ⓓ Vigor Graphic Design, LLC. Ⓒ Mark Garrison Salon

4A Ⓓ Thomas Manss & Company Ⓒ Cutcost.com   4B Ⓓ Polemic Design Ⓒ Ralph Appelbaum Associates   4C Ⓓ Lisa Speer Ⓒ Twistology   4D Ⓓ Brandia Ⓒ Galp Energia

5A Ⓓ Lesniewicz Associates Ⓒ Step-by-Step   5B Ⓓ Thomas Manss & Company Ⓒ Infineon   5C Ⓓ Stiles+co Ⓒ LogLogic   5D Ⓓ Eric Baker Design Assoc. Inc Ⓒ verb Interactive

84

A	B	C	D	
pharmaco **G** enomics™	astra lodge	Biokorntakt	Jantzen	1
barcode	mad river post	p**⊙**wersquid	tigo	2
fuse	ec**⊙**ffice	n·able	redfish	3
HUMAN RIGHTS CANADIAN MUSEUM FOR	AMNES¹A LEST WE FORGET	TWIS⊥	CHANGE OF SPACE	4
CREACTIVO	ARSENICO	NOTORIOUS	PIVOTAL FITNESS	5

	A	B	C	D
1	EROICA	MIYAKE	SEE-USA	FIVEPOINT
2	LUCINA	Skwish fun classic	BAYSIDE MARKET	WORLD UNCORKED
3	christmas	MARIXA	RIVALS	SBANE
4	MIKEY	It's happening in ALASKA	PUSH	BENT
5	SRTECE FTFSU NORTON TFSUF SECRET STUFF ERSCET FUFTS TERECS UFTSF	NEW YORK PUBLIC LIBRARY DONNELL BRANCH	HŌM	CODA

D = Design Firm   C = Client

1A D Sharp Communications, Inc. C Eroica Partners LLC   1B D Ali cindoruk C Arredamento Mimarlik   1C D Kym Abrams Design C SEE-USA   1D D Lisa Starace C fivepoint

2A D morrow mckenzie design C Shauna Mohr   2B D Werner Design Werks C Skwish for Manhattan Toy Company   2C D Miriello Grafico, Inc. C Boney's Bayside Market   2D D Edward Allen C World Uncorked

3A D Stiles+co C Christmas   3B D Modern Dog Design Co. C Marixa   3C D Playoff Corporation C Rivals   3D D www.iseedots.com C Hawkins Creative Services

4A D David Kampa C Texas Monthly   4B D batesneimand C Alaska Coalition   4C D CAPSULE C The PUSH Institute   4D D Sandstrom Design C BENT

5A D Gee + Chung Design C Symantec Corporation   5B D Polemic Design C Proposal   5C D Interrobang Design Collaborative, Inc. C HOM Interior Design   5D D Justin Johnson C Cody Johnson

B
Identity Design

Miles Newlyn, London, United Kingdom

Miles Newlyn's logo design is as different from the mainstream as it could possibly be. It challenges clients and designers alike. That's because of the unique angle from which he views the field. He cites a quote from Jung in *Man and His Symbols:*

"A word or image is symbolic when it implies something more than its obvious and immediate meaning. It has a wider 'unconscious' aspect that is never precisely defined or explained . . . . As the mind explores the symbol, it is led to ideas that lie beyond the grasp of reason."

The quote explains a lot to the London-based Newlyn. "What I find great about the quote is that you can forget any definition of what a logo is and consider anything as a logo, if it is saying what you want it to. In the context of branding, for example, an auto manufacturer's cars *are* its primary symbol. The cars are the corporate communication. This is the reason why auto manufacturers have adopted almost photographic rendering of their badges/mascots for their logos," Newlyn says. Logos don't appear in viewers' minds as flat things, rather just as things.

To create a logo for B, a prospective brand for a mobile communications business in the Seychelles, the designer had this in mind. After researching the Seychelles, a scattering of lush tropical islands in the Indian Ocean, Newlyn became interested in the coco de mer, an ancient palm tree unique to the islands. The trees produce the so-called love nut, a symbol so important that it is featured on the local currency. The shape was an appropriate and evocative connection to the islands.

"What might a service company's rendering of its imaginary mascot look like? Also, companies increasingly see themselves as a destination: not what you are buying, but where it takes you," the designer says.

Working with long-time collaborator Ali Coleman, Newlyn crafted a form that is many things: the letterform *B,* a suggestion of the form of the coco de mer nut, and all sorts of sexually provocative shapes. The form is decidedly three-dimensional and full of energy, representing the company's locus as communications provider within this small community.

In designing a new logo, it's crucial not only to represent the client but also to understand the client's audience. "Much of what I do is typographic, so it's important to understand how various people feel about letter styles. Different audiences see different things. These nuances are often a source of inspiration to either build upon or react against. A business for which I'm creating a logo may want to be considered a part of a nation, or it may not," Newlyn says. "B decidedly needed to be connected to its home.

"The solution gained the client's confidence in our understanding their audience, and it also opened their eyes to a creative experience. In this sense, the logo was accepted. Clients often take the rare opportunity of their branding project as an enjoyable experience with the creative industry, and not all branding projects have to end with a protectable asset," says Newlyn. "I like this way of working, and if the client decides to implement strategies and visuals I've worked on, that's a bonus."

LOGO SEARCH

Keywords | **Enclosures**

Type: ○ Symbol ○ Typographic ○ Combo ● All

1

2

3

4

5

D = Design Firm   C = Client

1A D Modern Dog Design Co. C Brown Paper Tickets 1B D SKOOTA C Whiteleaf (proposed) 1C D Peterson & Company C University of Texas at Dallas School of Management 1D D Kern Design Group C North Castle Partners

2A D NeoGine Communication Design Ltd C City Print Communication 2B D Parachute Design C IVY Hotel + Residence 2C D GSD&M C Austin Museum of Art 2D D Landkamer Partners, Inc. C Epigram

3A D Edward Allen C La Zona Rosa 3B D www.iseedots.com C The Castle Group 3C D FutureBrand C Avianca Colombia 3D D Duffy & Partners C Thymes

4A D Visual Inventor Ltd. Co. C Digimedia 4B D Sandstrom Design C Fuse 4C D Pix Design, inc. C Union Market 4D D LogoDesignSource.com C INKI

5A D judson design associates C Story Films 5B D Dr. Alderete C Spatium magazine 5C D strategyone C Airgate International 5D D Mirko Ilic Corp C Spread, Inc

	A	B	C	D
1				
2				
3				
4				
5				

ⓓ = Design Firm　ⓒ = Client

A	B	C	D	
				1
				2
				3
				4
				5

Ⓓ = Design Firm   Ⓒ = Client

1A Ⓓ Living Creative Design Ⓒ WOWOW Entertainments Inc.   1B Ⓓ Ammunition Ⓒ Joe Public Relations Ltd   1C Ⓓ The Collaboration Ⓒ The Collaboration   1D Ⓓ Living Creative Design Ⓒ Korea IT Network

2A Ⓓ sheean design Ⓒ Pyramid Creative Studios   2B Ⓓ Alphabet Arm Design Ⓒ Eric Klein   2C Ⓓ Parachute Design Ⓒ RMF Group   2D Ⓓ David Kampa Ⓒ Penny's Pastries

3A Ⓓ morrow mckenzie design Ⓒ Carafe   3B Ⓓ Fauxkoi Ⓒ Lily Red   3C Ⓓ Lars Lawson Ⓒ The Damien Center   3D Ⓓ The Flores Shop Ⓒ Gridlock Paintball Team

4A Ⓓ Idea Girl Design Ⓒ Nasty's   4B Ⓓ R&R Partners Ⓒ Atomic Testing Museum   4C Ⓓ greteman group Ⓒ cosmic cocktails   4D Ⓓ Werner Design Werks Ⓒ Style Stretch

5A Ⓓ Dan Rood Design Ⓒ John Hutton   5B Ⓓ Stephan and Herr Ⓒ Fleer   5C Ⓓ UNO Ⓒ Target Stores   5D Ⓓ Shift design Ⓒ PTM

	A	B	C	D

1

 LOGO SEARCH

Keywords **Display Type**

Type: ○ Symbol ○ Typographic ○ Combo ● All

 (1C)

 (1D)

2

 (2A)

 (2B) oxlo systems

 (2C) AMAZE

Champions (2D)

3

flick (3A)

 post: (3B)

pod (3C)

marvin (3D)

4

reduce it (4A)

ak9demy (4B)

 lava (4C)

toboggan (4D)

5

 one (5A)

 GO (5B)

 buiLD (5C)

 100 VEGAS CENTENNIAL 2005 (5D)

ⓓ = Design Firm   ⓒ = Client

1C ⓓ S4LE.com ⓒ ruby Cruz Ultimate 1D ⓓ David Kampa ⓒ Private Clubs Magazine

2A ⓓ rajasandhu.com ⓒ Edge Link 2B ⓓ (twentystar) ⓒ Oxlo Systems 2C ⓓ rajasandhu.com ⓒ rajasandhu.com 2D ⓓ David Kampa ⓒ Reebok

3A ⓓ Iperdesign, Inc. ⓒ Nish-Shinjuko, Tokyo 3B ⓓ KURT FOR HIRE ⓒ Multiverse 3C ⓓ GetElevatedDesign.com ⓒ People of Diversity 3D ⓓ Blue Studios, Inc. ⓒ Marvin

4A ⓓ Idea Girl Design ⓒ Reduce It 4B ⓓ judson design associates ⓒ k9 Academy 4C ⓓ Lance Reed ⓒ MAF 4D ⓓ Dialekt Design ⓒ Toboggan Design

5A ⓓ Special Modern Design ⓒ one world 5B ⓓ Felixsockwell.com ⓒ hasbro 5C ⓓ joe miller's company ⓒ Businesses United in Investing, Lending, & Development 5D ⓓ R&R Partners ⓒ Las Vegas Convention & Visitors Authority

A B C D

    1

    2

    3

   4

  5

A   B   C   D

1

2

3

4

5

Ⓓ = Design Firm   Ⓒ = Client

1A Ⓓ Steven O'Connor Ⓒ maca 76 1B Ⓓ Chimera Design Ⓒ MOMAC 1C Ⓓ Mirko Ilic Corp Ⓒ darkwood dub 1D Ⓓ Soho Joe Ⓒ KidWise Institute, Inc.

2A Ⓓ Strategy Studio Ⓒ Dub Rogers Photography 2B Ⓓ Gridwerk Ⓒ CTN Solutions 2C Ⓓ Garfinkel Design Ⓒ BITS Bunney IT Services 2D Ⓓ Banowetz + Company, Inc. Ⓒ GLAAD

3A Ⓓ Dr. Alderete Ⓒ Gratarola magazine 3B Ⓓ Lisa Starace Ⓒ Chango Macho Hot Sauces 3C Ⓓ Schuster Design Group Ⓒ Visionworks 3D Ⓓ Brandia Ⓒ TAP Portugal

4A Ⓓ Edward Allen Ⓒ The National Pastime 4B Ⓓ Werner Design Werks Ⓒ Long John Silver's 4C Ⓓ Catch Design Studio Ⓒ CATCH 4D Ⓓ pleitezgallo:: design haus Ⓒ La Sierra U. Church

5A Ⓓ Gardner Design Ⓒ Epic Apparel 5B Ⓓ Owen Design Ⓒ Art 316 5C Ⓓ J6Studios Ⓒ 2AM 5D Ⓓ Stuph Clothing Ⓒ Toby Mac

1

  2

  3

  4

  5

Ⓓ = Design Firm   Ⓒ = Client

1A Ⓓ Sayles Graphic Design, Inc. Ⓒ House of Bricks Bar & Grille 1B Ⓓ Werner Design Werks Ⓒ VH1 1C Ⓓ Alphabet Arm Design Ⓒ Or Music 1D Ⓓ Studio Stubborn Sideburn Ⓒ Stubborn Sideburn

2A Ⓓ Edward Allen Ⓒ KAOS-kids are our specialty 2B Ⓓ Banowetz + Company, Inc. Ⓒ Advanced Placement Strategies 2C Ⓓ Hubbell Design Works Ⓒ Ten Restaurant

2D Ⓓ Gabriel Kalach * V I S U A L communication Ⓒ Arrso Restaurants Co. 3A Ⓓ Sommese Design Ⓒ Joe Junk 3B Ⓓ David Kampa Ⓒ The Alley Theatre 3C Ⓓ Peterson & Company Ⓒ Kinexus Kinetic Museum

3D Ⓓ Steve's Portfolio Ⓒ Biblos 4A Ⓓ rajasandhu.com Ⓒ Spoiled Rotten Entertainment 4B Ⓓ Gardner Design Ⓒ Fringe Salon 4C Ⓓ soupgraphix Ⓒ Split clothing 4D Ⓓ David Kampa Ⓒ Live Oak Brewing Company

5A Ⓓ David Kampa Ⓒ Loophole Entertainment 5B Ⓓ CONCEPTiCONS Ⓒ Roger Espinoza 5C Ⓓ maximo, inc. Primas de la Viña LLC 5D Ⓓ Whence: the studio Ⓒ Finestra

R&D Thinktank
Identity Design

Tom Nynas, Dallas, Texas

R&D Thinktank is a young ad agency, located in Dallas, founded in 2001 by Doug Rucker and Jan Deatherage, both veterans of The Richards Group. Their goal was to create a company where clients could acquire full-service capabilities to build their brands, but with a high level of senior involvement that larger ad agencies have trouble maintaining. R&D Thinktank aims to be a complete advocate: friendly, concerned, forward-thinking.

"This group wanted to do things differently: They are a think tank, coming at the best solutions from all angles, not a traditional studio or ad group," explains Tom Nynas.

A cold, conventional monogram logo or corporate symbol would not be appropriate for this new creative approach. The letters *R&D* also presented their own problems because they could easily be misconstrued to mean "research and development" (they actually stand for Rucker and Deatherage). In the end, the team found the ambiguity a fun double meaning and embraced its possibilities.

Nynas, who at the time of this logo design project was a designer at another studio, considered a number of illustrated solutions that were decidedly unconventional—a light bulb brain, a tank with a thought bubble emerging from its gun, and a light bulb with a fish inside.

"This was a visual client, pretty savvy with respect to what they wanted, so I was able to present a number of unusual ideas," Nynas says.

Interpreting the word *tank* literally seemed to be a promising direction, although the military tank was quickly deemed inappropriate and the fish tank/light bulb felt cliché. So Nynas began thinking about tanks from other angles.

A scuba tank was an intriguing idea. This tank provides life-giving air, and its user is an adventurous explorer. "You need air to survive. An agency survives on ideas. So ideas are an agency's oxygen," Nynas says.

The designer drew an unforgettable and unconventional logo: a scuba diver with a brain as an air tank. The client loved the logo, and the mark soon came to life in other ways. The diver quickly became known as Jacques. Today, R&D has a big fish tank in its office entry. It offers a Jacques Award for employees who embody creative excellence, no matter which discipline they represent within the agency. Account and creative people alike have been recipients of the Jacques Award.

"The logo has really taken on a life of its own that we did not anticipate," says Nynas, who has since been hired by R&D Thinktank as director of design.

LOGO SEARCH

Keywords: **Calligraphy**

Type: ○ Symbol ○ Typographic ○ Combo ● All

Vaughan

Wrapsody

Harbour SUITES

Anasazi RESTAURANT

Sandman

Sprouts

Lavender

Disfigure

Lewis and Clark

Spanish Walk

Barefoot

Sundance MIND & BODY THERAPY

Johnny Reno

Las Vegas

Seanachai

Fly LABEL

	A	B	C	D
1		cosmetic café *the spirit of authentic beauty*	haute tuna	the martha's vineyard african-american film festival
2	Sun Tropics	Jasper's	Fresh™ Get Set for Home Décor	PROVINCIA DE Buenos Aires
3			Schoc chocolatier	Sukra Yoga
4		JAZZ	Zoe	
5				

Ⓓ = Design Firm   Ⓒ = Client

1A Ⓓ Felixsockwell.com Ⓒ firefly 1B Ⓓ Insight Design Ⓒ Cosmetic Café 1C Ⓓ judson design associates Ⓒ Haute Tuna 1D Ⓓ adbass:designs LLC Ⓒ cobblestoneentertainment grp.

2A Ⓓ Brandesign Ⓒ Sun Tropics 2B Ⓓ Banowetz + Company, Inc. Ⓒ Kent Rathbun/Jasper's Restaurant 2C Ⓓ Goldforest Ⓒ QEP Co. 2D Ⓓ FutureBrand Ⓒ Buenos Aires Provincial Government

3A Ⓓ Lisa Starace Ⓒ ocotillo 3B Ⓓ Dirty Design Ⓒ Noveau Filth 3C Ⓓ NeoGine Communication Design Ltd Ⓒ Schoc Chocolatier 3D Ⓓ Kendall Ross Ⓒ Sukra Yoga

4A Ⓓ Keyword Design Ⓒ Towle Community Theater 4B Ⓓ FUSZION Collaborative Ⓒ United States Conference of Mayors 4C Ⓓ CONCEPTiCONS Ⓒ Zoe-Miniature Schnauzer 4D Ⓓ Starlight Studio Ⓒ Miranda Movies

5A Ⓓ GSCS Ⓒ UAE royal family 5B Ⓓ Sakkal Design Ⓒ M. Al Meer, Dubal 5C Ⓓ Sakkal Design Ⓒ Hedgebrook Foundation 5D Ⓓ Sakkal Design Ⓒ Tahrir Literary Project

LOGO SEARCH

Keywords: **Crests**

Type: ◯ Symbol   ◯ Typographic   ◯ Combo   ⦿ All

ⅅ = Design Firm   ⒸG = Client

1C ⅅ judson design associates ⒼG Kountry Bakery 1D ⅅ sheean design ⒼG Deutsch/LA Advertising
2A ⅅ Sayles Graphic Design, Inc. ⒼG Des Moines Jaycees 2B ⅅ Parachute Design ⒼG Lusso Exclusive Residence Collection 2C ⅅ IMAGEHAUS ⒼG Ron Beining 2D ⅅ Colle + McVoy ⒼG CHS
3A ⅅ Sockeye Creative ⒼG adidas 3B ⅅ Entemotion Design Studio Small Town Treasures 3C ⅅ Barnstorm Creative Group Inc ⒼG Mark James Restaurants 3D ⅅ HMK Archive ⒼG Mitch Webb & the Swindles
4A ⅅ Sandstrom Design ⒼG Full Sail 4B ⅅ Fauxkoi ⒼG anodyne bev co. 4C ⅅ Olson + Company ⒼG Outdoor Corps 4D ⅅ R&R Partners ⒼG Ministry of Productivity
5A ⅅ Gardner Design ⒼG Fringe Salon 5B ⅅ Gardner Design ⒼG Renewed 5C ⅅ Gardner Design ⒼG aspen traders 5D ⅅ dedstudios ⒼG ecouture

	A	B	C	D
1				
2				
3				
4				
5				

⊅ = Design Firm   ⊂ = Client

1A ⊅ Sibley Peteet ⊂ Kenny Wayne Shepherd   1B ⊅ Gardner Design ⊂ Renewed   1C ⊅ Delikatessen ⊂ Club Nobel   1D ⊅ Gardner Design ⊂ Renewed

2A ⊅ UNO ⊂ Target   2B ⊅ eindruck design ⊂ Ceres Bakery   2C ⊅ Design and Image ⊂ Kamala   2D ⊅ dotzero Design ⊂ Oasis at Bermuda Dunes

3A ⊅ Wolken communica ⊂ Avec Amis Event Planning   3B ⊅ PowerGroove Creative Outwest   3C ⊅ Ryan Cooper ⊂ Network Solutions   3D ⊅ Design and Image ⊂ Deborah Williams

4A ⊅ Gardner Design ⊂ The Lone Ranger   4B ⊅ Garfinkel Design ⊂ Bee Natural   4C ⊅ Wholesale Distributors ⊂ Lucid Inc.   4D ⊅ Gardner Design ⊂ Bradley Paper

5A ⊅ Gardner Design ⊂ Bradley Paper   5B ⊅ judson design associates ⊂ Divas   5C ⊅ sheean design ⊂ Unfiltered Napa   5D ⊅ Suburban Utopia ⊂ Downtown Athens Recording Company

100

	A	B	C	D	
1					1
2	(LA COSTA RIDGE)	PEDDIE SCHOOL	(CONEY ISLAND)	(THE COMMONS PIERPONT)	2
3	(H·E·B ANNIVERSARY 100 YEARS)	(MANY HANDS CRAFTERS)	(RANDALL FARMS BEEF)	(PAXICO SAUSAGE)	3
4	(ORNAMINTS)	(passport to europe)	(SIERRA TAP HOUSE)	(THE JOSHUA EXPERIENCE)	4
5	(PULP CULTURE)	(RALEIGH SPY CONFERENCE)	(BAUER FIRST LINE DEALER)	(Backroads TRAVELER.com)	5

	A	B	C	D

D = Design Firm   C = Client

LOGO SEARCH

Keywords: **Sports**

Type: ◯ Symbol ◯ Typographic ◯ Combo ● All

PEST WORLD SERIES

	A	B	C	D
1				
2				
3				
4				
5				

Ⓓ = Design Firm   Ⓒ = Client

1A Ⓓ Paul Black Design Ⓒ National Hole in One Association   1B Ⓓ The Oesterle Ⓒ The Golf Room   1C Ⓓ b5 Marketing & Kommunikation GmbH Ⓒ GreenSports   1D Ⓓ Jeff Pollard Design Ⓒ Nike

2A Ⓓ Hope Advertising Ⓒ Priddis Greens   2B Ⓓ Edward Allen Ⓒ Bandon Dunes   2C Ⓓ Edward Allen Ⓒ Paloma Loca/Lyon Advertising   2D Ⓓ Brand Navigation Ⓒ Puerto Luperon

3A Ⓓ Mode Design Studio Ⓒ KT40.com   3B Ⓓ marc usa Ⓒ Indpls Sports corp   3C Ⓓ Fredrik Lewander Ⓒ Sprtnik   3D Ⓓ Hanna & Asssociates Ⓒ Spokane Hoopfest

4A Ⓓ Sockeye Creative Ⓒ adidas   4B Ⓓ morrow mckenzie design Ⓒ Nike   4C Ⓓ David Kampa Ⓒ Nike   4D Ⓓ David Kampa Ⓒ Nike

5A Ⓓ Rickabaugh Graphics Ⓒ Big East Conference   5B Ⓓ Rickabaugh Graphics Ⓒ Ball Hawg   5C Ⓓ Turney Creative Ⓒ Shirts & Skins Basketball   5D Ⓓ Turney Creative Ⓒ Shirts & Skins Basketball

	A	B	C	D

    1

    2

    3

    4

    5

Ⓓ = Design Firm   Ⓒ = Client

1A Ⓓ Glitschka Studios Ⓒ Kimberly-Clark Worldwide   1B Ⓓ The Joe Bosack Graphic Design Co. Ⓒ Youngstown Steelhounds   1C Ⓓ Barnstorm Creative Group Inc Ⓒ MayDay Marketing

1D Ⓓ Barnstorm Creative Group Inc Ⓒ Main Events Boxing   2A Ⓓ greteman group Ⓒ pivotal fitness   2B Ⓓ synergy Graphix Ⓒ Spring Brothers   2C Ⓓ o2 ideas Ⓒ Vulcan Run

2D Ⓓ The Clockwork Group Ⓒ North Central Rotary Club/San Antonio   3A Ⓓ Chimera Design Ⓒ Tennis Victoria   3B Ⓓ DDB Dallas Ⓒ Susan G. Komen Breast Cancer Foundation   3C Ⓓ humanot Ⓒ STFC

3D Ⓓ Eyebeam Creative LLC Ⓒ America Scores   4A Ⓓ ComGroup Ⓒ ADT   4B Ⓓ Lars Lawson Ⓒ USA Diving   4C Ⓓ Lars Lawson Ⓒ USA Diving   4D Ⓓ Brainding Ⓒ Western

5A Ⓓ The Joe Bosack Graphic Design co. Ⓒ Unused   5B Ⓓ HMK Archive Ⓒ Randall Mays   5C Ⓓ Ross Hogin Design Ⓒ Cutter & Buck   5D Ⓓ Sayles Graphic Design, Inc. Ⓒ American Athletic Incorporated

2003 INAS-FID International Football Tournament
Identity Design

Brandia, Lisbon, Portugal

Players in the annual INAS-FID (International Sports Federation for Persons with Intellectual Disability) international football tournament are required to have certain qualifications in addition to superior soccer-playing skills: They must also have doctors' reports attesting to their mental illness or learning disability. Sponsored by two national associations that support those afflicted with mental illness or related disabilities, the tournament is well known in Portugal.

"The Federation is a non-profit whose main purpose is to develop and organize the practice of sports in a competitive environment for Portuguese athletes who bear mental illnesses," explains Miguel Reis, a design director from Brandia, a Lisbon-based design office that was asked to design a logo for the 2003 games.

In 2003, the scope of the games had spread due to testimonials from famous soccer players from around the world. Therefore, the new logo had to express not only the event but its worldwide presence. The notion of different peoples coming together was even more important to note. Not only were people of many nationalities playing together, but so were people of differing disabilities.

"The games have a diversity of cultures, of ways of life and feelings," explains Reis. The designer experimented with silhouettes of people, but this idea was discarded as too open to interpretation. Another idea that was explored was hands in many colors. But this could be interpreted in a patronizing way—that the participants need special help.

"We abandoned that idea because we thought we should emphasize the strongest part of the games, the differences," the designer says.

The solution is a soccer ball that looks as though it could be forming or coming apart. Its many transparent colors play off each other in abstract ways, but the overall shape is still recognizable. The idea is to show dynamism and the many ways a single entity—be it a ball or a person—can be interpreted.

"The concept is that of the importance of each part in the formation of a strong whole. The actual form does not matter; the differences do not matter. The important factor is the clear and transparent way of assuming the differences between each part and its importance in the whole," Reis says.

The logo is powerful and faithful to the concept of the tournament. It is light and transparent in its construction but strong in its final form.

LOGO SEARCH

Keywords: **Heads**

Type: ○ Symbol ○ Typographic ○ Combo ● All

🅳 = Design Firm   🅲 = Client

1C 🅳 ZEBRA design branding 🅲 Union of Russian Designers 1D 🅳 ZEBRA design branding 🅲 Rubberman

2A 🅳 Studio Simon 🅲 New Hampshire Primaries 2B 🅳 FUSZION Collaborative 🅲 Addys 2C 🅳 Glitschka Studios 🅲 Work Labs 2D 🅳 tesser 🅲 Yum Brands - KFC

3A 🅳 Steven O'Connor 🅲 Capleton 3B 🅳 Sockeye Creative 🅲 Digital One 3C 🅳 GRAF d'SIGN creative boutique 🅲 High Fidelity 3D 🅳 MEME ENGINE 🅲 ANYISM

4A 🅳 Formikula 🅲 Marc Herold 4B 🅳 Studio Stubborn Sideburn 🅲 Stubborn Sideburn 4C 🅳 KURT FOR HIRE 🅲 Angry Waiter 4AM 4D 🅳 9fps 🅲 9 Frames Per Second

5A 🅳 Kahn Design 🅲 Ultimate Rider 5B 🅳 Diagram 🅲 Von Der Heyden Group 5C 🅳 Brainding 🅲 Matchstrike 5D 🅳 Mattson Creative 🅲 Maroon5

	A	B	C	D
1				
2				
3				
4				
5				

A	B	C	D	
				1
				2
				3
				4
				5

	A	B	C	D
1				
2				
3				
4				
5				

A	B	C	D	
				1
				2
				3
				4
				5

1A Ⓓ thehappycorp global Ⓒ the happycorp global 1B Ⓓ Les Kerr Creative Ⓒ DynaZeck Technologies 1C Ⓓ Mindspike Design, LLC Ⓒ Dr. James Magestro, Orthodontist 1D Ⓓ David Maloney Ⓒ Brain Magnet

2A Ⓓ Diagram Ⓒ Ink Design Studio 2B Ⓓ Brainding Ⓒ Papamedia 2C Ⓓ Vincent Burkhead Studio Ⓒ Collabora Design 2D Ⓓ Brainding Ⓒ Interpretext

3A Ⓓ J6Studios Ⓒ Flip Sounds 3B Ⓓ GSCS Ⓒ Noshi Noshi 3C Ⓓ sharp pixel Ⓒ joe nation 3D Ⓓ V V N Design Ⓒ Brainy Broads

4A Ⓓ Tim Frame Design Ⓒ Tom Maloney 4B Ⓓ Special Modern Design Ⓒ Hype Public Relations 4C Ⓓ Exti Dzyn Ⓒ Egad Dzyn 4D Ⓓ HMK Archive Ⓒ RailYard Productions

5A Ⓓ HMK Archive Ⓒ Wild Blue Yonder Entertainment 5B Ⓓ INNFUSION Studios Ⓒ A Maad Tea Party 5C Ⓓ Mariqua Design Ⓒ Lucy Lane 5D Ⓓ Entermotion Design Studio Ⓒ Ad Salon

	A	B	C	D
1				
2				
3				
4				
5				

1A Ⓓ UNO Ⓒ TOO   1B Ⓓ Howling Good Designs Ⓒ Jodi Richards   1C Ⓓ NeoGine Communication Design Ltd Ⓒ Schoc Chocolatier   1D Ⓓ GingerBee Creative Ⓒ Joy Publications

2A Ⓓ The Clockwork Group Ⓒ Foresight Consulting   2B Ⓓ Ramp Ⓒ Richard Schafer   2C Ⓓ Macnab Design Visual Communication Ⓒ Self/Symbol literacy project   2D Ⓓ Brainding Ⓒ Criterion

3A Ⓓ i3design Ⓒ Todd Mc Feely   3B Ⓓ Peterson & Company Ⓒ See Pictures   3C Ⓓ Banowetz + Company, Inc. Ⓒ Kim Dawson Talent Agency   3D Ⓓ Chimera Design Ⓒ City of Port Phillip

4A Ⓓ Werner Design Werks Ⓒ Media Minds, Inc.   4B Ⓓ Idle Hands Design Ⓒ Hollyfield   4C Ⓓ Strange Ideas Ⓒ Brain Bank   4D Ⓓ Turner Duckworth Ⓒ Greenberg Research

5A Ⓓ Special Modern Design Ⓒ Hype   5B Ⓓ Boelts/Stratford Associates Ⓒ Smile Works   5C Ⓓ Brandia Ⓒ Galp Energia   5D Ⓓ GRAF d'SIGN creative boutique Ⓒ MetaCosmetic

Blue Q/Hot & Flashy
Identity and Product Design

Haley Johnson Design, Minneapolis, Minnesota

Haley Johnson Design is a leader in the growing trend of designers working as product creators, not just as product designers. Since the launch of the delectably scented Dirty Girl brand in 1999, the design studio has launched nine successful personal care brands for a single client—Blue Q—the latest of which is Hot & Flashy.

"It was meant to be a menopausal brand," says Haley Johnson, laughing a bit at the notion of creating a design for this niche market. "I was concerned about making this a product line more widely accepted in the gift market. I was uncomfortable focusing totally on menopause, but at the same time I needed to fulfill the desires of the demographic."

Johnson interviewed women in the forty-five- to fifty-five-year-old age group, but it was a twenty-one-year-old niece who really put things into perspective for her. "She told me that sometimes she feels old," the designer recalls. "I realized that no matter the hormone level, every woman needs to be revitalized once in a while. You don't have to be menopausal to need a boost."

For the brand identity, Johnson began by considering what feeling the words *hot* and *flashy* should portray. For the target group,

she decided that letterforms that expressed energy and power would be appropriate. All of Johnson's product designs are highly stylized, usually by time period. For this design, she felt the Art Deco era would be a good match.

"The women of that time appear liberated, sophisticated, and strong in their new-found industrial age. That intrigued me. The richness of the color and design from that period seemed right for the Hot & Flashy demographic, too. It's more mature and opulent, not girly or trendy," she says.

Johnson's typography is an authentic take on the Art Deco period, while its color makes it modern. It and the accompanying graphics are full of contrasts, with plenty of dynamic deco details.

For color, the designer followed the lead of each product. Each item has a unique palette with hot accents and flashy copper metallic foil. For instance, the energy supply kit plays with shades of blue and a spark of yellow. The soap has neutral shades of brown with a hit of lime green.

Overall, the Hot & Flashy identity is cool and confident, just like the women to whom the product is meant to appeal.

LOGO SEARCH

Keywords **People**

Type: ○ Symbol ○ Typographic ○ Combo ◉ All

  LAS Links

1

2

3

4

5

	A	**B**	**C**	**D**
1				
2				
3				
4				
5				

1

2

3

4

5

A   B   C   D

	A	B	C	D
1				
2				
3				
4				
5				

Ⓓ = Design Firm   Ⓒ = Client

1A Ⓓ greteman group Ⓒ art 101   1B Ⓓ Straka Dusan Ⓒ Festundfrei eK   1C Ⓓ Dotzero Design Ⓒ Kritis   1D Ⓓ Dotzero Design Ⓒ PCM

2A Ⓓ FUSZION Collaborative Ⓒ F&W Publications   2B Ⓓ Insight Design Ⓒ Single Source   2C Ⓓ The Gate Ⓒ HelaCapital   2D Ⓓ Richards Brock Miller Mitchell & Associates Ⓒ Champion Contractors

3A Ⓓ Visual Inventor Ltd. Co. Ⓒ Tulsa Radiology Associates/Visionmakers   3B Ⓓ cc design Ⓒ Narcissus   3C Ⓓ 9MYLES, Inc. Ⓒ Alignment in Motion   3D Ⓓ Bronson Ma Creative Ⓒ Inner City Relief

4A Ⓓ Strange Ideas Ⓒ secret perfume   4B Ⓓ Dotzero Design Ⓒ Polish Festival   4C Ⓓ Werner Design Werks Ⓒ VH1 Networks   4D Ⓓ Diagram Ⓒ Wedliniarnia Meat Delicatessen

5A Ⓓ HMK Archive Ⓒ Sabas Trio International   5B Ⓓ GS&M Ⓒ Joy Moves   5C Ⓓ zwölf sonnen Ⓒ Einwohner-und Integrationsamt Wiesbaden   5D Ⓓ Lance Reed Ⓒ Soho

118

	A	B	C	D	

1

2

3

4

5

D = Design Firm   **C** = Client

1A **D** joven orozco design **C** Barcode Guys 1B **D** Campbell Fisher Design **C** Pot Heads 1C **D** humanot **C** Unseen Kings 1D **D** Wolken communica **C** Just Cauz

2A **D** DDB Dallas **C** Milton Development Company 2B **D** Communique **C** Foster the Future 2C **D** (twentystar) **C** Colorado Ridge Church 2D **D** zwölf sonnen **C** Peter Kohl

3A **D** Launchpad Creative **C** Daisy Group 3B **D** Monster Design Company **C** Milkdrunk Baby 3C **D** Idle Hands Design **C** Luna Ladder Art for Productions, LLC 3D **D** Glitschka Studios **C** Glitschka Studios

4A **D** Gabi Toth **C** Conti Grup Romania 4B **D** M3 Advertising Design **C** Chris Hammond 4C **D** Studio D **C** Glen Burtnik 4D **D** Who's the Min / Creative Solutions **C** BandCamp Productions

5A **D** Mattson Creative **C** Vital Dynamics 5B **D** i4 Solutions **C** Ron Williams 5C **D** Farm Design **C** Street Jammy Jam Series 5D **D** J6Studios **C** Houston Area Knife Stickers

	A	B	C	D
1				
2				
3				
4				
5				

A B C D

1

2

3

4

5

	A	B	C	D
1				
2				
3				
4				
5				

🅓 = Design Firm   🅒 = Client

1A 🅓 Howerton+White Interactive 🅒 Maternal Fetal Associates of Kansas   1B 🅓 Strange Ideas 🅒 connect mate   1C 🅓 elf design 🅒 Weddings   1D 🅓 Felixsockwell.com 🅒 AIDS

2A 🅓 Straka Dusan 🅒 residential home for the elderly   2B 🅓 Straka Dusan 🅒 FirstFootStep   2C 🅓 BrandSavvy, Inc. 🅒 Double Angel Foundation   2D 🅓 FUSZION Collaborative 🅒 abyan.com

3A 🅓 Shelley Design + Marketing 🅒 Parents Anonymous   3B 🅓 UNO 🅒 Kimberly Clark   3C 🅓 traci jones design 🅒 Hearts for Forgotten Angels   3D 🅓 Sommese Design 🅒 Children's Playschool

4A 🅓 monster design 🅒 Microsoft Alumni Association   4B 🅓 Macnab Design Visual Communication 🅒 Insight Out   4C 🅓 Kevin France Design, Inc. 🅒 You're Not Alone   4D 🅓 o2 ideas 🅒 Quorum

5A 🅓 Special Modern Design 🅒 Flewelling & Moody Architects   5B 🅓 McAndrew Kaps 🅒 Associated Pension Service   5C 🅓 Peterson & Company 🅒 ERF   5D 🅓 Lesniewicz Associates 🅒 Marrow Donor

A	B	C	D	
				1
				2
				3
				4
				5

	A	B	C	D
1				
2				
3				
4				
5				(Clayscapes Pottery)

A　　　　　　B　　　　　　C　　　　　　D

    　1

    　2

    　3

    　4

    　5

D = Design Firm　　**C** = Client

1A **D** Univisual **C** VistaSi　1B **D** Macnab Design Visual Communication **C** Body Wisdom Day Spa　1C **D** mccoycreative **C** HandsOn Salon　1D **D** FigDesign **C** Webb Chiropractic

2A **D** Think Tank Creative **C** Acadiana Open Channel　2B **D** Jenny Kolcun Freelance Designer **C** Ojo Photography　2C **D** Peterson & Company **C** Women's National Book Association　2D **D** Jeff Pollard Design **C** Digitech Solutions

3A **D** Fuego3 **C** Dove Counseling Services　3B **D** Harkey Design **C** Harkey Design　3C **D** FUSZION Collaborative **C** CADCA　3D **D** Glitschka Studios **C** Glitschka Studios

4A **D** Atha Design **C** Oskaloosa Elementary PTO　4B **D** Gabriela Gasparini Design **C** Colby & Partners　4C **D** Glitschka Studios **C** GloveMobile.com　4D **D** Kahn Design **C** Kathy Taylor/Acupuncture & Chinese Herbalist

5A **D** Felixsockwell.com **C** Cigna　5B **D** IMA Design, Corp. **C** Club Portfelio　5C **D** Felixsockwell.com **C** Cigna　5D **D** Idea Girl Design **C** Special Olympics

Operation Seneca
Identity Design

Crescent Lodge, London, United Kingdom

The design team at Crescent Lodge (London) was asked by the Metropolitan Police Service to create a strong yet reassuring identity for Operation Seneca. This strategic initiative is a collaboration of the police and London bus companies that aims to reduce crime levels on the city's public transportation routes.

Information gathered via inward—and outward—facing electronic surveillance equipment on London's buses and police training buses is being used to combat crime and keep the public safe. Named for Lucius Annaeus Seneca, the philosopher and statesman who tried to solve the problems caused by Rome's disaffected youth, the operation, it is hoped, will become associated with public-spirited vigilance.

Designer David Lovelock led the project at Crescent Lodge. "Originally, our idea for the logo was inspired by the welcoming sight of a brightly lit double-decker bus on a dark city night. The shape of the glowing bus windows gives the finished identity its structure. The bus itself remains as unobtrusive as the surveillance undertaken by Operation Seneca."

The logo was given its first airing when the Metropolitan Police Service made a series of presentations to London bus companies in order to persuade them to become partners in the effort. At this writing, several police training buses bearing Operation Seneca livery are in circulation. Parked at strategic points throughout London, they are helping gather intelligence, facilitate swift responses when crimes are committed, and raise awareness among Londoners of this important initiative.

"The London bus is a familiar, much-loved icon. By turning it into a beacon of light and associating it with a surveillance operation aimed at controlling crime and protecting people, we have created a robust identity that is positive and comforting rather than threatening or oppressive. These days, Londoners are less inclined to object to the growing presence of surveillance cameras anyway, so Operation Seneca and the logo that represents it are very much in tune with the times."

If the success of an initiative like Operation Seneca can be measured by the amount of funding raised to continue its good work, it is worth noting that a state-of-the-art Transport Command Unit is now up and running, thanks to a Transport for London-backed grant of £47 million.

LOGO SEARCH

A **B** **C** **D**

Keywords [**Mythology**]

Type: ○ Symbol   ○ Typographic   ○ Combo   ● All

1

NAUGHTY
&
NICE

COLLECTION

2

INFLUENCE

3

HALL of
INFAMY

4

BEWARE
BAD IDEAS!

HELLBILLIES

AUSTIN, TEXAS

THE BLACK PEARL

5

TRIATHLETE
ZOMBIES

FRIGHTTOWN

ⓓ = Design Firm   ⓒ = Client

1C ⓓ Iperdesign, Inc. ⓒ De Carolis Jewelry 1D ⓓ Farah Design, Inc. ⓒ Farah Design

2A ⓓ V V N Design ⓒ Influence 2B ⓓ Sommese Design ⓒ Penn State Jazz Club 2C ⓓ KW43 BRANDDESIGN ⓒ Ritzenhoff AG 2D ⓓ Sabingrafik, Inc. ⓒ Hot Rod Hell

3A ⓓ Scott Oeschger Design ⓒ Scott Oeschger 3B ⓓ Tactix Creative ⓒ Work Labs 3C ⓓ GSD&M ⓒ Tobacco Beast 3D ⓓ Werner Design Werks ⓒ i-Village

4A ⓓ Tactix Creative ⓒ www.BadDesignKills.com 4B ⓓ Glitschka Studios ⓒ BadDesignKills.com 4C ⓓ Edward Allen ⓒ Hellbillies 4D ⓓ Zed+Zed+Eye Creative Communications ⓒ Matt Villella

5A ⓓ Glitschka Studios ⓒ Haro Bikes 5B ⓓ sheean design ⓒ Triathlete Zombies 5C ⓓ Novasoul ⓒ Legion 5D ⓓ Dotzero Design ⓒ FrightTown

	A	B	C	D
1				
2				
3				
4				
5				

A   B   C   D

    1

     2

    3

    4

    5

Ⓓ = Design Firm   Ⓒ = Client

1A Ⓓ CAPSULE Ⓒ Myth Nightclub   1B Ⓓ McAndrew Kaps Ⓒ Wavecode   1C Ⓓ Gardner Design Ⓒ Spirit Aerosystems   1D Ⓓ Tactical Magic Ⓒ Fulmer Helmets

2A Ⓓ Hinge Ⓒ Internet2   2B Ⓓ ivan2design Ⓒ Kharakat   2C Ⓓ Harkey Design Ⓒ Griffin Company   2D Ⓓ David Kampa Ⓒ Horsefeathers Trading Company

3A Ⓓ Quest Fore Ⓒ GlaxoSmithKline   3B Ⓓ Element Ⓒ Columbus School for Girls   3C Ⓓ Diagram Ⓒ ING Real Estate Development   3D Ⓓ Sergio Bianco Ⓒ Incisori Fiorentini

4A Ⓓ Idle Hands Design Ⓒ Ouroboros Ink   4B Ⓓ Turner Duckworth Ⓒ S.A. Brain & Co. Ltd   4C Ⓓ Glitschka Studios Ⓒ Body Glove-Asia   4D Ⓓ Studio Simon Ⓒ Golden Baseball League

5A Ⓓ the atmosfear Ⓒ MGM MIRAGE   5B Ⓓ www.iseedots.com Ⓒ NovaStor   5C Ⓓ sheean design Ⓒ Maddocks & Co.   5D Ⓓ Sommese Design Ⓒ Penn State Jazz Club

	A	B	C	D
1				
2				
3				
4				
5				

Ⓓ = Design Firm   Ⓒ = Client

1A Ⓓ Ramp Ⓒ Kelston International   1B Ⓓ Diagram Ⓒ ING Real Estate Development   1C Ⓓ Tim Frame Design Ⓒ Crashshop   1D Ⓓ ASGARD Ⓒ Shell Company 78

2A Ⓓ Rotor Design Ⓒ Ames Children's Theater   2B Ⓓ Fuze Ⓒ akaKeen   2C Ⓓ Werner Design Werks Ⓒ Aether for Nike   2D Ⓓ Tactix Creative Ⓒ Boat Locker

3A Ⓓ Glitschka Studios Ⓒ Rearden Studio   3B Ⓓ Glitschka Studios Ⓒ Publisher   3C Ⓓ Glitschka Studios Ⓒ Publisher   3D Ⓓ Glitschka Studios Ⓒ Publisher

4A Ⓓ Dr. Alderete Ⓒ Heineken Mexico   4B Ⓓ Fuego3 Ⓒ Fuego3   4C Ⓓ Tactix Creative Ⓒ Moki's   4D Ⓓ Fifth Letter Ⓒ Ooga Booga!, Inc.

5A Ⓓ Glitschka Studios Ⓒ Upper Deck Company   5B Ⓓ Chad Carr Design Ⓒ Space Cat   5C Ⓓ CONCEPTiCONS Ⓒ Migdia Chinea   5D Ⓓ Strange Ideas Ⓒ pop robot icon

Bravo Network
Identity Redesign

Open, New York, New York

Bravo is the only television network whose name makes a statement. It's something one might actually say out loud, particularly in response to the arts programming it carried at its inception some twenty years ago.

Its logo was a straightforward affair until recently, when Open (New York City) redesigned it as part of an overall redesign of the network. Since NBC bought Bravo in 2003, the network has gone through a series of changes.

Bravo used to be a general arts channel, with movies, interviews with authors, concerts—a PBS that wasn't PBS, explains Scott Stowell, the proprietor of Open. "Since NBC took over, they've run shows like *Queer Eye for the Straight Guy, Celebrity Poker Showdown,* and reruns of *West Wing.* It's a real hodgepodge," he says.

More recently, Bravo has added original shows like the popular *Project Runway*, and a tagline, "Watch what happens," that celebrates the variety of programming on the network. So the Bravo logo had to make a statement, too, expressing the reaction to seeing something surprising and great.

The Canadian version of Bravo has an exclamation point at the end of its wordmark. It was a small jump for the designers to add a word bubble to the U.S. version. "It was an obvious idea," Stowell says, "but the response from the client was positive."

But getting to the final logo took a lot more fine-tuning. Color and type studies were conducted for weeks and weeks. The new logo

had to look fresh but be similar enough to the original mark that loyal viewers would feel comfortable with it. Tobias Frere-Jones of Hoefler & Frere-Jones Typography drew the type for the final logo.

The shape of the word bubble required its own set of extensive studies. "Our favorite version was a rectangle. One of the client's mandates was to attract more male viewers—hence, the hard, angled shape. But Bravo felt that might be too generic, and they asked that we make a shape that could be more specific," Stowell says.

After many experiments with shapes, corners, line weight, and so on, Bravo president Lauren Zalaznick asked that the designers try placing two rounded corners on one end and two right angles on the other. It worked, both as an effective word bubble shape and as a strong identifier. The final design is definitely specific to Bravo.

Stowell feels the logo succeeds because it is so simple. It's what it is supposed to be. "It fulfills the requirements of a classic logo. It's not 3-D or made of metal or translucent. It can be run in a flat color or stitched onto a baseball hat or silkscreened onto a shirt. Many logos today are more like illustrations because they're so complicated," he adds. "This one works really well inside the busy environment of TV."

(Top) New design
(Bottom) Old design

LOGO SEARCH

Keywords **Birds**

Type: ◯ Symbol ◯ Typographic ◯ Combo ⦿ All

A	B	C	D	
		JARDINI		1
MINE™				2
			Serbian Refugee Council	3
		Access Knowledge		4
nest egg PAPERS		Baby	nest egg papers	5

	A	B	C	D
1				
2				
3				
4				
5				

Ⓓ = Design Firm   Ⓒ = Client

1A Ⓓ R&D thinktank Ⓒ AwakeTel   1B Ⓓ Steven O'Connor Ⓒ chicken   1C Ⓓ Gardner Design Ⓒ Backroads Traveler   1D Ⓓ Colle + McVoy Ⓒ Ciatti's Chianti Grill

2A Ⓓ ivan2design Ⓒ El Pollo Loco   2B Ⓓ Morse and Company Advertising Communications Ⓒ Cyrano's Restaurant   2C Ⓓ Element Ⓒ Howe Family Reunion 2005   2D Ⓓ Whence: the studio Ⓒ The Krewe of Wild Turkeys

3A Ⓓ KONG Design Group Ⓒ Listen Skateboards   3B Ⓓ Rick Johnson & Company Ⓒ Quail Ranch   3C Ⓓ Dashwood Design Ltd Ⓒ Farrow Jamieson   3D Ⓓ Sandstrom Design Ⓒ White Owl

4A Ⓓ Bright Strategic Design Ⓒ Paradise on a Hanger   4B Ⓓ Gardner Design Ⓒ Bradley Paper   4C Ⓓ Gardner Design Ⓒ Bradley Paper   4D Ⓓ Fernandez Design Ⓒ Kiwi

5A Ⓓ McGuire Design Ⓒ Denise Swanson   5B Ⓓ Gardner Design Ⓒ City of Newton, KS   5C Ⓓ Michael Courtney Design, Inc. Ⓒ Maggie Martin, Midwife   5D Ⓓ Mires Ⓒ Pelican Video Games

LOGO SEARCH

Keywords **Fish/Bugs/Reptiles**

Type: ⚪ Symbol   ⚪ Typographic   ⚪ Combo   ⦿ All

	A	B	C	D	
1					1
2					2
3					3
4					4
5					5

ⓓ = Design Firm   ⓒ = Client

1C ⓓ M3 Advertising Design ⓒ Osaka Sushi   1D ⓓ Diagram ⓒ Aqua Park Sopot

2A ⓓ Perfect Circle Media Group ⓒ Tekno Sushi Bar   2B ⓓ GSD&M ⓒ fishdirectory.com   2C ⓓ Fredrik Lewander ⓒ Johan Broman   2D ⓓ Hubbell Design Works ⓒ Fashionfish

3A ⓓ Strange Ideas ⓒ Aquatic Concepts   3B ⓓ David Kampa ⓒ Blue Fish Development Group   3C ⓓ Naughtyfish ⓒ one fish two fish kidswear and maternity   3D ⓓ urbanINFLUENCE design studio ⓒ ticklefish

4A ⓓ The Logo Factory Inc. ⓒ Puff Nation Clothing   4B ⓓ Red Circle ⓒ kung fu fish   4C ⓓ Strange Ideas ⓒ Flaming Lures   4D ⓓ Fernandez Design ⓒ Flying Fish

5A ⓓ PosterV.Design Studio ⓒ Enqua Ltd.   5B ⓓ www.iseedots.com ⓒ Mike Stelzner   5C ⓓ Lunar Cow ⓒ Safelite Solutions   5D ⓓ Mindgruve ⓒ Cal Mar

	A	B	C	D
1				
2				
3				
4				
5				

Ⓓ = Design Firm   Ⓒ = Client

1A Ⓓ Sergio Bianco Ⓒ Valter Franco Ricci 1B Ⓓ Peak Seven Advertising Ⓒ Waterside 1C Ⓓ Mad Dog Graphx Ⓒ Ukpeagvik Inupiat Corporation 1D Ⓓ Tom Fowler, Inc. Ⓒ The Maritime Aquarium at Norwalk

2A Ⓓ dale harris Ⓒ renega 2B Ⓓ Ammunition Ⓒ August.One Communications 2C Ⓓ The Robin Shepherd Group Ⓒ Grippers Surf Wax 2D Ⓓ FUSZION Collaborative Ⓒ The Caribbean

3A Ⓓ Glitschka Studios Ⓒ Upper Deck Company 3B Ⓓ The Robin Shepherd Group Ⓒ J. Johnson Gallery 3C Ⓓ Strange Ideas Ⓒ Nautilus Pictures 3D Ⓓ Cato Purnell Partners Ⓒ UniSuper

4A Ⓓ ZEBRA design branding Ⓒ IVS Group 4B Ⓓ Glitschka Studios Ⓒ Upper Deck Company 4C Ⓓ Cato Purnell Partners Ⓒ Britz Rentals 4D Ⓓ Lesniewicz Associates Ⓒ China Stone

5A Ⓓ Glitschka Studios Ⓒ Upper Deck Company 5B Ⓓ Dotzero Design Ⓒ Kritis 5C Ⓓ Glitschka Studios Ⓒ Upper Deck Company 5D Ⓓ Farm Design Shop-o-saurus

A	B	C	D	
		beyond blue		1
	THE ART STATION *Growth & Healing Through the Creative Arts*	 BETTER ATM		2
				3
				4
				5

ⒹⒹ = Design Firm　ⒼⒼ = Client

1A Ⓓ Gardner Design Ⓖ Plastic Surgery Center　1B Ⓓ Sommese Design Ⓖ Lauth Development　1C Ⓓ Cato Purnell Partners Ⓖ beyond blue　1D Ⓓ Alphabet Arm Design Ⓖ G2G Management
2A Ⓓ Gardner Design Ⓖ Plastic Surgery Center　2B Ⓓ Brian Blankenship Ⓖ The Art Station　2C Ⓓ Tactix Creative Ⓖ Better ATM Services　2D Ⓓ Thomas Manss & Company Ⓖ Ability International
3A Ⓓ Gardner Design Ⓖ Hustler　3B Ⓓ Bronson Ma Creative Ⓖ 1st American Bank　3C Ⓓ Farm Design Ⓖ Queen Bee Waxing　3D Ⓓ elf design Ⓖ Have Wax, Will Travel
4A Ⓓ Sayles Graphic Design, Inc. Ⓖ Busy Bee Tailoring　4B Ⓓ Gardner Design Ⓖ Hustler　4C Ⓓ jsDesignCo. Ⓖ buzzsaw.com　4D Ⓓ Ross Hogin Design Ⓖ Buzzbee
5A Ⓓ Banowetz + Company, Inc. Ⓖ Hotel ZaZa　5B Ⓓ Banowetz + Company, Inc. Ⓖ Hotel ZaZa　5C Ⓓ Felixsockwell.com Ⓖ firefly　5D Ⓓ judson design associates Ⓖ Linda and Jim Goodnight

137

Skywest
Identity Design

Cato Purnell, Sydney and Melbourne, Australia

Lead people on a journey from evolution to revolution: that's what Graham Purnell's team wanted to do when it created a new logo and identity for Skywest, a small regional airline in Western Australia, where air travel is a geographic necessity. Miles and miles of outstanding landscape and implied adventure lie between points: Skywest could tell consumers how thought-provoking the journey could be for business and tourism travelers alike.

"We wanted to push the boundaries for the client and for the traveler," says Purnell, creative director of Cato Purnell Partners, Sydney and Melbourne.

Skywest had to deal with stiff competition from better-known airlines such as Virgin Blue. But it also had the opportunity to move into dead center and deliver a more emotional message, one that was unique to the feeling of being in Australia.

Purnell's team started with givens: the client's name and choice of color, which really had to be a sky blue.

"Skywest is a great name. We wanted the new identity to open up the concept of *sky*. In Western Australia, there is this broad expanse of sky," Purnell says. He and his designers developed a frame element roughly 3.5 times wider than it is tall that is a crucial part of the new identity. In it, the blue sky can appear, or panoramic shots from any Skywest destination can be dropped in. "The box is iconic and strong on its own. It is a revolutionary concept of panorama."

Another important part of the new identity is a sunburst. "When you look out the plane window, you often see this sunflower light on the glass. The sunburst element is distinctive and new in the industry. Now, they can take a panoramic shot of a tourist destination, put it in the frame, then stamp it with the sunburst in order to take ownership, so to speak, of the destination," Purnell explains.

LOGO SEARCH

Keywords **Animals**

Type: ○ Symbol ○ Typographic ○ Combo ● All

UNDERDOG
ANIMATION

bowhouse

BraggingRightsonline
"It Pays To Be The Top Dog"

doglogic
AGILITY·TRAINING

THE PALMS
PET RESORT & SPA

A B C D

1 2 3 4 5

ⓓ = Design Firm   ⓒ = Client

1C ⓓ Jon Flaming Design ⓒ Dog's Day 1D ⓓ Elephant In The Room ⓒ Doglogic

2A ⓓ judson design associates ⓒ Underdog Animation Studio 2B ⓓ retropup ⓒ Bowhouse 2C ⓓ The Clockwork Group ⓒ Bragging Rights Online 2D ⓓ Launchpad Creative ⓒ OKC Yard Dogs

3A ⓓ Glitschka Studios ⓒ Upper Deck Company 3B ⓓ Elephant In The Room ⓒ doglogic 3C ⓓ Simon & Goetz Design ⓒ HS Fashion 3D ⓓ DDB Dallas ⓒ The Dog House

4A ⓓ ROBOT ⓒ The Palms Pet Resort and Spa 4B ⓓ Banowetz + Company, Inc. ⓒ Frenkel & Frenkel 4C ⓓ Blue Studios, Inc. ⓒ Bingo Broadband 4D ⓓ Brandia ⓒ Galp Energia

5A ⓓ FUSZION Collaborative John Guilt 5B ⓓ Rick Johnson & Company ⓒ The Bone Bistro 5C ⓓ Savage Design Group ⓒ The Black Labrador 5D ⓓ Sockeye Creative ⓒ Lucky Labrador Brewing Company

139

	A	B	C	D
1				
2				
3				
4				
5				

Ⓓ = Design Firm   Ⓒ = Client

1A Ⓓ amyHELLER design Ⓒ Paws Gourmet, Inc   1B Ⓓ Hausch Design Agency LLC Ⓒ Jeanette Kebisek   1C Ⓓ Visual Inventor Ltd. Co. Ⓒ Three Legged Dog   1D Ⓓ Type G Ⓒ Lucky Dog Pet Boutique

2A Ⓓ Insomniac Creative Studio Ⓒ Hattie Larlham/Constant Companions   2B Ⓓ Macnab Design Visual Communication Ⓒ Animal Medical Clinic   2C Ⓓ C. Cady Design Ⓒ Critter Sitters   2D Ⓓ Edward Allen Ⓒ Humane Society of Austin

3A Ⓓ Sommese Design Ⓒ Pet Extravaganza   3B Ⓓ NeoGine Communication Design Ltd Ⓒ Schoc Chocolatier   3C Ⓓ angryporcupine*design Ⓒ Zombiecat Productions   3D Ⓓ Diagram Ⓒ Cat Children's Clothing

4A Ⓓ Blue Storm Design Ⓒ ByStorm   4B Ⓓ Eyescape Ⓒ Liongate Capital Management   4C Ⓓ Gardner Design Ⓒ Material Comforts   4D Ⓓ Gardner Design Ⓒ Fringe Salon

5A Ⓓ Brandia Ⓒ Sporting Clube de Portugal   5B Ⓓ Harwood Kirsten Leigh McCoy Ⓒ La Casa Re   5C Ⓓ Sabet Branding Ⓒ Walid Mahmoud   5D Ⓓ Werner Design Werks Ⓒ Cheetah Valley

A   **B**   **C**   **D**

1

2

3

4

5

1A Ⓓ Honey Design Ⓒ Auburn Developments   1B Ⓓ Uhlein Design Ⓒ Fox Chase Homeowners Association   1C Ⓓ Paul Black Design Ⓒ Howard Wolf   1D Ⓓ Kinesis, Inc. Ⓒ MTILDA

2A Ⓓ Ikola designs... Ⓒ International Species Information System   2B Ⓓ R&D Thinktank Ⓒ Rams   2C Ⓓ Gardner Design Ⓒ Hustler   2D Ⓓ Campbell Fisher Design Ⓒ The Phoenix Zoo

3A Ⓓ Oxide Design Co. Ⓒ Springbok   3B Ⓓ Bonilla Design Ⓒ Wild Game, Inc.   3C Ⓓ Deep Design Ⓒ Macauley Companies   3D Ⓓ Lesniewicz Associates Ⓒ Owens Corning

4A Ⓓ Zipper Design Ⓒ Mini Doe Boutique   4B Ⓓ Sibley Peteet Ⓒ SMAM/Hunt Realty   4C Ⓓ Sabingrafik, Inc. Ⓒ Rocky Mountain Elk Foundation   4D Ⓓ Ikola designs... Ⓒ Minnesota Zoological Society

5A Ⓓ Lesniewicz Associates Ⓒ Erie Bleu Alpaca Farm   5B Ⓓ Strategic America Ⓒ Horsepower Energy Drink   5C Ⓓ Hill Design Studios Ⓒ Red Fence Farm   5D Ⓓ Sayles Graphic Design, Inc. Ⓒ Wildwood Hills Ranch

	A	B	C	D
1				
2				
3				
4				
5				

A	B	C	D	
				1
				2
				3
				4
				5

	A	**B**	**C**	**D**
1				
2				
3				
4				
5				

ⓓ = Design Firm ⓒ = Client

Domaine Restaurants Ltd.
Identity Design

Ramp Creative, Los Angeles, California

The logo and identity system for Domaine Restaurants Ltd., a holding company in Orange County, California, that owns and creates progressive and highly regarded restaurants, is an excellent example of a successful compromise.

Ramp Creative, Los Angeles, was the design firm that achieved the bargain. Principals Michael Stinson and Rachel Elnar met with Domaine owners Tim and Liza Goodell, who together have founded nationally recognized restaurants such as Meson G, Troquet, and Aubergine. Right away, the designers saw that the partners could easily head in different directions in their new identity. Tim, a talented French chef, loved traditional concepts. Liza, on the other hand, wanted a modern design, full of color and personality.

Stinson and Elnar did design experiments that ranged from pole to pole—traditional to modern—but they soon discovered that the two could be blended, much to the pleasure of the clients. The logo solution was a traditional, illuminated letterform, a combination of a D and an R intertwined with vines and ivy.

"The mark is ornate, like ivy climbing over a passageway opening in France, leading to a tunnel that goes into a vineyard," says Stinson.

But the way the logo was implemented in the identity was very modern. On one side of Domaine's calling card-sized business cards (2 ½" x 3 ½" [6.35 x 8.89 cm]) is the engraved logo on a chocolate-brown field. But on the other side is a bright mint-green field with the card carrier's contact information. Other pieces in the system carried other bright colors.

"We did a whole palette for them. The rest of the stationery utilized a salmon color for the envelopes and a lime green for the letterheads. The company folders' neutral palette accommodated the bright colors used inside as well as on the website. The brown color ties everything together; it allows all the colors in the system to be joined by this neutral color," explains Stinson. This flexibility is important because Domaine operates many styles of restaurant, traditional and contemporary. The identity must serve as an accommodating umbrella for all of them.

The ivy element in the logo turned out to be another contemporary element on Domaine's website (www.domainerestaurants.com). Ramp Creative animated the tendrils so they wind and twine on different pages. But rather than displayed in black or a solid color, they are transparent, allowing new images to show through from behind. The effect obscures and reveals at the same time. Ramp even shot all the imagery that appears on the website to ensure the visuals coordinated with the modern feel of the site.

"When we first met with Tim and Liza, they argued like two chefs. They definitely had two different styles, but this blend works for them both," Stinson says.

LOGO SEARCH

Keywords | **Nature**

Type: ⦾ Symbol ◯ Typographic ◯ Combo ⦿ All

A **B** **C** **D**

1

2

3

4

5

	A	B	C	D	
		 			1
					2
					3
					4
					5

	A	B	C	D

1

Kansas Stars

ZŁOTE TARASY

Bubel
Aiken
foundation

2

agave

ilove.com

3

SUNJOI

NUANSA ASRI CIPADU

4

DAILY*colors*™

BOTANIA

North American Biomass Corporation

5

INN AT BEVERLY HILLS

CORHAM

PROSPECT
PLACE
apartments

PICO
MACCARIO

Ⓓ = Design Firm   Ⓒ = Client

1A Ⓓ Carol Gravelle Graphic Design Ⓒ Tournesol Siteworks 1B Ⓓ Strange Ideas Ⓒ Kansas Stars 1C Ⓓ Diagram Ⓒ ING Real Estate Development 1D Ⓓ Anoroc Ⓒ Bubel Aiken Foundation
2A Ⓓ Mattson creative Ⓒ Centex Homes 2B Ⓓ juls design inc Ⓒ The Iowa Clinic 2C Ⓓ Shawn Hazen Graphic Design Ⓒ Self 2D Ⓓ Sterling Brands Ⓒ America Online
3A Ⓓ Cato Purnell Partners Ⓒ Flower Factory 3B Ⓓ ROBOT Ⓒ SunJoi Corporation 3C Ⓓ Armeilia Subianto Design Ⓒ Nuansa Asri Cipadu 3D Ⓓ Boom Creative Ⓒ Neighborhood Lawn Care
4A Ⓓ Bright Strategic Design Ⓒ Daily Colors 4B Ⓓ Strange Ideas Ⓒ Botania 4C Ⓓ B.L.A. Design Company Ⓒ NABC 4D Ⓓ Gardner Design Ⓒ Material Comforts
5A Ⓓ Banowetz + Company, Inc., Ⓒ Inn at Beverly Hills 5B Ⓓ Zombie Design Ⓒ Corham Company 5C Ⓓ octane inc. Ⓒ JB Communications 5D Ⓓ Sergio Bianco Ⓒ Pico Maccario

A	B	C	D	
POPPYSEED CAKE INVITATIONS · CARDS	FRANCE JACMAIN STYLIST		jardín	1
		CASTLEWOOD at BIG SKY	Каракулино Молоко ®	2
seed™	Europharm		EUROCATALYST EVERYBODY WINS	3
	GOURMONDO the art of food		CONIFER PURVEYORS of SPECIALTY FOODS	4
			Asah Terra	5

Ⓓ = Design Firm   Ⓒ = Client

1A Ⓓ elf design Ⓒ Poppyseed Cake 1B Ⓓ Ardoise Design Ⓒ Immotik inc. 1C Ⓓ GetElevatedDesign.com Ⓒ Green Lotus Grounds 1D Ⓓ Lisa Starace Ⓒ jardín

2A Ⓓ baba designs Ⓒ Enchanted Minstrel Music 2B Ⓓ The Pink Pear Design Company Ⓒ Idlewild Jewelry Design 2C Ⓓ Mattson Creative Ⓒ Shea Homes 2D Ⓓ design-studio Muhina Ⓒ Karakulino Milk

3A Ⓓ seed Ⓒ seed 3B Ⓓ Brandient Ⓒ GlaxoSmithKline 3C Ⓓ Imaginaria Ⓒ Azteca Milling 3D Ⓓ HMK Archive Ⓒ euroCatalyst

4A Ⓓ Rickabaugh Graphics Ⓒ Mountain View Coffee Roasters 4B Ⓓ Methodologie Ⓒ Gourmondo Catering 4C Ⓓ zwölf sonnen Ⓒ Förderverein Fachhochschule Wiesbaden 4D Ⓓ Brand Navigation Ⓒ Conifer Specialties

5A Ⓓ Gardner Design Ⓒ The Lone Ranger 5B Ⓓ The Flores Shop Ⓒ The Cedarhouse School 5C Ⓓ Richards Brock Miller Mitchell & Associates Ⓒ The Home Depot 5D Ⓓ Curtis Sharp Design Ⓒ Asah Terra

	A	B	C	D
1				
2				
3				
4				
5				

Ⓓ = Design Firm   Ⓒ = Client

1A Ⓓ OmniStudio Inc Ⓒ Modern Africa   1B Ⓓ Ramp Ⓒ compLife   1C Ⓓ Hinge Ⓒ Bonsai Labs   1D Ⓓ Miriello Grafico, Inc. Ⓒ Barratt American

2A Ⓓ Mohouse Design Co. Ⓒ Lakewood Service League   2B Ⓓ Actual Size Creative Ⓒ Shady Grove   2C Ⓓ Napoleon design Ⓒ APAE-Associação de Pais e Amigos dos Excepcionais-Bauru   2D Ⓓ Sibley Peteet Ⓒ Sanders\Wingo

3A Ⓓ www.iseedots.com Ⓒ Orchard Group, Inc.   3B Ⓓ The Collaboration Ⓒ City of Glendale   3C Ⓓ The Robin Shepherd Group Ⓒ Earth Day   3D Ⓓ Diagram Ⓒ Plantec

4A Ⓓ Felixsockwell.com Ⓒ Cigna   4B Ⓓ Simon & Goetz Design Ⓒ Elenxis   4C Ⓓ Brandia Ⓒ BancoBIC   4D Ⓓ christiansen : creative Ⓒ liveliberal.org

5A Ⓓ joe miller's company Ⓒ Shade   5B Ⓓ the zen kitchen Ⓒ Branches Fine Gifts   5C Ⓓ concussion, llc Ⓒ Treehouse Foods, Inc.   5D Ⓓ judson design associates Ⓒ Chinquapin School

A	B	C	D	
				1
				2
				3
				4
				5

Ⓓ = Design Firm   Ⓒ = Client

	A	B	C	D
1				
2				
3				
4				
5				

D = Design Firm C = Client

Froggy
Identity Redesign

Zebra Design Branding, Togliatti, Russia

Froggy is a Russian computer product that allows customers to order new computers à la carte—that is, users tell a Froggy specialist what they want to do with the computer, and the specialist pulls together the most appropriate configuration using parts from leading component manufacturers, including Intel and Samsung. Users can also decide how much power their computer needs, selecting from one of five comprehensive RAM levels.

Froggy, a division of IVS Group in Perm, is known as a friendly brand, ideal for the person who wants to use a computer for games, the Internet, and word processing but who knows little about electronics. The company's old logo had a friendly enough look: a smiling, T-shirt-wearing cartoon frog that sat still for print applications and was animated for electronic media. Once only a home computer brand, Froggy moved into the business market as well, and the old logo was no longer appropriate.

The client even wondered if the company name should be changed. But Andrey Mitin, art director of Zebra Brand Marketing (Togliatti, Russia) didn't think so. "In our opinion, the name Froggy is the most accurate way to show the character of this brand, its essence. A froggy is a kind and positive character. It is never mischievous or troublesome, nor are Froggy computers," he says.

Still, Mitin and his designers wanted to address the client's concerns about whether or not a frog was too whimsical for its expanding business. So they dissected the frog, so to speak, and considered elements of the creature that would reflect the company's friendly nature yet be decidedly more corporate.

The wide-open, bubblelike eyes of a frog were considered, but the frog foot held even more potential. It could be made simple and modern as a shape, yet speak of the original brand and animal.

"The basic meaning of the new logo is as a helping hand the froggy stretches out to everyone in a complicated computer world," explains Mitin. "Alongside the primary meaning, this logo can also be looked at as a tree—a principle of computer systemizing—or microcircuit contacts. Some people even see the famous USB symbol in it."

Using the color orange made the frog foot even more distinctive, as frogs this color are exotic and rare. The orange is unexpected and memorable. The bright, positive color is also a strong differentiating factor that distinguishes Froggy from duller, more corporate rivals.

The new brand positioning statement—"Play. Learn. Think. Work. Win!"—was released at the same time as the logo (in fact, it can sit right inside the new logo), and both have been a hit, and not just with customers. In February 2005, the Froggy brand earned the right to carry Microsoft's "Designed for Windows" statement on its products and packaging. The new identity was also ranked in the top ten of the best-rated corporate identities in Russia for 2005.

The new logo and identity immediately received positive public reaction. Contact with the brand is much more pleasant, for customers and staff. Since the new launch, Froggy has attracted more corporate customers and has extended its segment of home users. Rebranding helped the company become a leader in the personal computer market in Perm, says Mitin.

LOGO SEARCH

Keywords | **Shapes**

Type: ○ Symbol   ○ Typographic   ○ Combo   ● All

	A	B	C	D
1			ASSURANT	**BankDirect**
2		WORLDWIDE OPERATIONS	**grupo H**	x·cursion
3		AIRWAVE		MUNDO SPORTING VIAGEM AO UNIVERSO LEONINO
4	PURL.	Centigon	TerryWhite chemists	OCEANIA
5	4° INAS-FID Campeonato de Futebol EURO'03			Davidson Oil

Ⓓ = Design Firm   Ⓒ = Client

1C Ⓓ Carbone Smolan Agency Ⓒ Assurant   1D Ⓓ Cato Purnell Partners Ⓒ Bank Direct

2A Ⓓ David Kampa Ⓒ David Carter Design   2B Ⓓ Gee + Chung Design Ⓒ Sun Microsystems   2C Ⓓ Brainding Ⓒ grupo H   2D Ⓓ Gardner Design Ⓒ X-Cursion

3A Ⓓ Strategy Studio Ⓒ International Resource Center   3B Ⓓ R&R Partners Ⓒ Airwave   3C Ⓓ Fernandez Design Ⓒ Citrix   3D Ⓓ Brandia Ⓒ Sporting Clube de Portugal

4A Ⓓ switchfoot creative Ⓒ Conquest Trading Co.   4B Ⓓ Landor Associates Ⓒ Centigon   4C Ⓓ Cato Purnell Partners Ⓒ Terry White Chemists   4D Ⓓ Strange Ideas Ⓒ Oceania

5A Ⓓ Brandia Ⓒ INAS FID   5B Ⓓ Thomas Manss & Company Ⓒ VCC Perfect Pictures   5C Ⓓ Shift design Ⓒ SDNM   5D Ⓓ tanagram partners Ⓒ Davidson Oil

Optimum
online

1

Simple
Software Training

tapspace creativity in percussion

REYES MARKETING

EQUITYMOMENTUM

2

Hydro Power

mood boost

Gforce

3

unison

4

MUSE 2005
Metropolitan University Scholar's Experience

ideal
exposure

5

	A	B	C	D
1	Arby's Franchise Association			
2	CLUSTER CONSULTING GROUP	Isix	QUEST SYSTEMS INC	fusion
3	ProteoPlex™	HYATT PLACE	FUSZION | COLLABORATIVE	
4	parago	evolutionemr simply advanced.		LEIDEN CROSS EFFECT LFE
5	bump networks	plusinfinite	mediaengine	Internal Monologue

1A Brand Bird Arby's   1B mattisimo pod interior design   1C Starlight Studio RM Custom Creations   1D Gee + Chung Design Art Center College of Design

2A Joi Design Cluster Consulting Group   2B tanagram partners Darc Corporation   2C Sutter Design Quest Systems   2D reduced fat John Zack

3A Justin Johnson ProteoPlex   3B Lippincott Mercer Hyatt Place   3C FUSZION Collaborative FUSZION Collaborative   3D Ross Hogin Design Connetics MMG

4A Bronson Ma Creative Parago, Inc.   4B d4 creative group Ethidium   4C Glitschka Studios Cyphon Design   4D A3 Design LFE

5A Brainding Bump networks   5B Brainding PlusInfinite   5C Grapefruit MediaEngine LLC   5D Interrobang Design Collaborative, Inc. Internal Monologue

A	B	C	D	
POLYSHELL	Listen In	goosebumps	**Valence** Health	1
	Netigy		cognistar	2
	Cálidda GAS NATURAL DEL PERÚ		Nowiejski 401(k) Associates, LP	3
			star *peer tutoring programme*	4
	pfi. Pink Films International			5

ⅅ = Design Firm Ⅽ = Client

1A ⅅ elaine park Ⅽ Akina Inc. 1B ⅅ bunch Ⅽ Listen In–Portugal 1C ⅅ Kaimere Ⅽ Goosebumps Records 1D ⅅ tanagram partners Ⅽ Valence Health

2A ⅅ Kym Abrams Design Ⅽ Montgomery Ward /Mobil 2B ⅅ Gee + Chung Design Ⅽ Netigy Corporation 2C ⅅ A3 Design Ⅽ New Jack Soul 2D ⅅ Lippincott Mercer Ⅽ Cognistar

3A ⅅ FutureBrand Ⅽ Buenos Aires Province Government 3B ⅅ FutureBrand Ⅽ Tractebel Peru 3C ⅅ Brian Blankenship Ⅽ Jetta 3D ⅅ Steven O'Connor Ⅽ Nowiejski 401(k) Associates, LP

4A ⅅ Braue; Branding & Corporate Design Ⅽ Concore 4B ⅅ Maremar Graphic Design Ⅽ Abbott Laboratories 4C ⅅ Letter 7 Ⅽ SixPointStudios 4D ⅅ Axiom Design Partners Ⅽ STAR Peer Tutoring Programme

5A ⅅ Landor Associates Ⅽ FedEx Kinko's 5B ⅅ Unibrand Belgrade Ⅽ pink film ⅅ Steven O'Connor Ⅽ EZLN 5D ⅅ S Design, Inc. Ⅽ Thinking Cap/Oklahoma Partnership for School Readiness

	A	B	C	D
1				
2				
3				
4				
5				

Ⓓ = Design Firm   Ⓒ = Client

1

2

3

4

5

Ⓓ = Design Firm   Ⓒ = Client

1A Ⓓ Sandstrom Design Ⓒ Surround Architects   1B Ⓓ Kendall Ross Ⓒ Precept Brands   1C Ⓓ NeoGine Communication Design Ltd Ⓒ Paragee   1D Ⓓ Cheri Gearhart, graphic design Ⓒ Sarah's Inn

2A Ⓓ Polemic Design Ⓒ Proposal   2B Ⓓ Jeff Pollard Design Ⓒ Cornish College of the Arts   2C Ⓓ Lippincott Mercer Ⓒ The Bank of New York   2D Ⓓ Cato Purnell Partners Ⓒ Clearview

3A Ⓓ Kineto Ⓒ PT Karya Deka Pancamurni   3B Ⓓ Gardner Design Ⓒ The Chapel   3C Ⓓ Brandia Ⓒ RadioTelevisão Portuguesa   3D Ⓓ 28 LIMITED BRAND Ⓒ Schleupen AG

4A Ⓓ Gardner Design Ⓒ Spirit Aerosystems   4B Ⓓ Visual Coolness Ⓒ Experience Analysts International   4C Ⓓ Gardner Design Ⓒ Spirit Aerosystems   4D Ⓓ Dashwood Design Ltd Ⓒ The EDGE

5A Ⓓ Mirko Ilic Corp Ⓒ Broadmoor Engineering   5B Ⓓ Barnstorm Creative Ⓒ Camelot Consulting   5C Ⓓ FutureBrand Ⓒ InBest Forex   5D Ⓓ Grapefruit Ⓒ UCS Romania

	A	B	C	D

1

2

3

4

5

Ⓓ = Design Firm   Ⓒ = Client

1A Ⓓ Braue; Branding & Corporate Design Ⓒ Thomas Marine Consultants 1B Ⓓ Velocity Design Works Ⓒ Pixelalbum 1C Ⓓ Onoma, LLC Ⓒ New York Terminals 1D Ⓓ Hutchinson Associates, Inc. Ⓒ Hutchinson Design Group

2A Ⓓ judson design associates Ⓒ Unused 2B Ⓓ CS Design Ⓒ xTech 2C Ⓓ 28 LIMITED BRAND Ⓒ Ulrich Volwinkel 2D Ⓓ Octane Ⓒ Alliance Commercial Real Estate

3A Ⓓ Brand Engine Ⓒ Propello 3B Ⓓ Aurora Design Ⓒ Mohawk Paper Mills 3C Ⓓ Lippincott Mercer Ⓒ DeVry 3D Ⓓ FutureBrand Ⓒ HSBC Argentina

4A Ⓓ Dashwood Design Ltd Ⓒ Fonterra 4B Ⓓ KW43 BRANDDESIGN Ⓒ Mannesmann Plastics Machinery 4C Ⓓ Sabet Branding Ⓒ Exagon 4D Ⓓ Letter 7 Ⓒ B2B Shipping Network

5A Ⓓ Shawn Hazen Graphic Design Ⓒ Bonk 5B Ⓓ Designsensory Ⓒ Sevier Heights Baptist Church 5C Ⓓ Glitschka Studios Ⓒ Ralston 360 5D Ⓓ Design MG Ⓒ for sale

LOGO SEARCH

A   **B**   **C**   **D**

Keywords **Symbols**

Type: ○ Symbol ○ Typographic ○ Combo ● All

1
2
3
4
5

Ⓓ = Design Firm   Ⓒ = Client

1C Ⓓ o2 ideas Ⓒ Crave Chocolatier 1D Ⓓ UltraVirgo Creative Ⓒ Polyamorous NYC

2A Ⓓ josh higgins design Ⓒ San Diego City College 2B Ⓓ Alphabet Arm Design Ⓒ Amanda Palmer 2C Ⓓ batesneimand Ⓒ The Fund for Animals 2D Ⓓ Sabingrafik, Inc. Ⓒ Trinchero Family Estates

3A Ⓓ R&R Partners Ⓒ New Vistas 3B Ⓓ A3 Design Ⓒ Dubois County Humane Society 3C Ⓓ Strategy Studio Ⓒ Christine's Fine Bake Goods 3D Ⓓ Howerton + White Interactive Ⓒ hart_1

4A Ⓓ Brainding Ⓒ Sante Coffee 4B Ⓓ Tactix Creative Ⓒ Invictus Group 4C Ⓓ Bryan Cooper Design Ⓒ American Heart Association 4D Ⓓ Rome & Gold Creative Ⓒ Amigo Fiel

5A Ⓓ Straka Dusan Ⓒ ProSiebenSat.1 Production 5B Ⓓ Straka Dusan Ⓒ proposal 5C Ⓓ ArtGraphics.ru Ⓒ Aqua Vision 5D Ⓓ UNO S Su-Frida

	A	B	C	D

1

2

3

4

5

1A Ⓓ Insight Design Ⓒ My Volunteer Center   1B Ⓓ Brainding Ⓒ Colliervielle   1C Ⓓ octane inc. Ⓒ Ultra Design   1D Ⓓ urbanINFLUENCE design studio Ⓒ Torrid Romance Publishers

2A Ⓓ Gardner Design Ⓒ Big Dog Motorcycles   2B Ⓓ Bronson Ma Creative Ⓒ 63 Ministry   2C Ⓓ Howling Good Designs Ⓒ headline communications   2D Ⓓ Gardner Design Ⓒ Ballet Wichita

3A Ⓓ Day Six Creative Ⓒ Eternal Oil & Gas   3B Ⓓ Chris Malven Design Ⓒ WestStreet Deli   3C Ⓓ Steven O'Connor Ⓒ open   3D Ⓓ Fox Parlor Ⓒ Parahamsa

4A Ⓓ Les Kerr Creative Ⓒ Trailblazer Studios   4B Ⓓ Parachute Design Ⓒ Sansei, Inc.   4C Ⓓ Metroparks of the Toledo Area Ⓒ Metroparks of the Toledo Area   4D Ⓓ Actual Size Creative Ⓒ Firehouse Lounge

5A Ⓓ A3 Design Ⓒ Hot Sake   5B Ⓓ Big Bald Guy Design Studio Ⓒ Benet Heating and Brazing   5C Ⓓ Fuego3 Ⓒ Fuego3   5D Ⓓ Curtis Sayers Design Ⓒ The MathWorks

	A	B	C	D

    1

    2

    3

    4

    5

🅓 = Design Firm   🅒 = Client

1A 🅓 Gabi Toth 🅒 Jester (UK) Limited   1B 🅓 Ditto! 🅒 Books for Boys   1C 🅓 Diagram 🅒 Swoboda Telecommunications   1D 🅓 Lienhart Design 🅒 Illinois Summer School for the Arts

2A 🅓 Paul Black Design 🅒 AquaStar Pools   2B 🅓 Gardner Design 🅒 Spectrum   2C 🅓 GSD&M 🅒 Texas Aerospace Consortium   2D 🅓 INNFUSION Studios 🅒 INNFUSION Studios

3A 🅓 Sandstrom Design 🅒 Converse   3B 🅓 concussion, llc 🅒 Texas Alliance of Dentists   3C 🅓 Mindspace 🅒 Armorworks   3D 🅓 switchfoot creative 🅒 Beach Hunter

4A 🅓 Gee + Chung Design 🅒 Sun Microsystems   4B 🅓 Jeff Pollard Design 🅒 Nike   4C 🅓 REINES DESIGN INC. 🅒 CONEKTA   4D 🅓 Fifth Letter 🅒 Enviro-Air Solutions

5A 🅓 Cato Purnell Partners 🅒 City Rail   5B 🅓 MEME ENGINE 🅒 PROJECT MOVEMENT   5C 🅓 Glitschka Studios 🅒 IMB - Fresh ID   5D 🅓 Brandia 🅒 GroundForce

	A	**B**	**C**	**D**
1				
2				
3				
4				
5				

Newslink
Identity Design

Hat-trick Design Consultants, London, United Kingdom

The success of Newslink's logo has as much to do with its initial design as it does with its consistent and effective implementation in direct mail, says Hat-trick Design art director Gareth Howat.

Newslink is a media product in the United Kingdom that allows radio advertisers to buy air immediate before and after newscasts, a period that elicits the highest levels of listener attention during the broadcast day. It is a premium product, somewhat costly, but very effective, says Howat.

Media buyers who might consider purchasing Newslink space are typically inundated with other buy options and promotions. So Newslink had to stand out in a simple and clear way in order to cut through the clutter.

"Media buyers get so much direct mail, a logo can only do so much to attract attention. Newslink's mailers and online environment, together with the logo, would be important in getting across key messages," the designer explains.

Howat began by exploring the notion of people who are listening, of sound waves, and of digital level bars that might be seen on sound control equipment. The client immediately embraced a concept in which the word *in,* already embedded in the name Newslink, was highlighted with color and brackets. Not only did the brackets frame the word in, they also resembled sound waves.

Framing *in* had another benefit: With expressions such as *in mind, in tune, in reach,* and *in depth,* the logo could be turned into its own changeable tagline.

"It's a flexible logo that we can change over time," Howat says of the mark, which today has five permutations. "It allows us to verbally pull out the core values of the product." The brackets device was also used to highlight other pieces of copy on key applications.

But Howat believes the direct mail Hat-trick created for Newslink made the logo come to life. The designs have a clean, visual style. The simpler and more direct, the better, he believes.

For example, Hat-trick created a card, printed in red and green, that was sent out with a red plastic filter that filtered out the red, cluttered text, representative of the overwhelming media noise that Newslink cuts out. The proof of the firm's approach was in the reaction of the mailer's approximately 5,000 recipients; it achieved an admirable 4.2 percent response where 0.5 percent is considered normal.

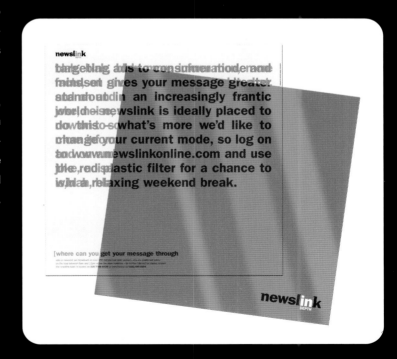

	A	B	C	D

A   B   C   D

LOGO SEARCH

1   Keywords [**Arts**]

Type: ○ Symbol   ○ Typographic   ○ Combo   ● All

2

3

4

5

	A	B	C	D
1				
2				
3				
4				
5				

Ⓓ = Design Firm   Ⓒ = Client

1A Ⓓ Rome & Gold Creative Ⓒ World-View Café   1B Ⓓ Fernandez Design Ⓒ Citrix   1C Ⓓ The Oesterle Ⓒ Micro Consult   1D Ⓓ Glitschka Studios Ⓒ Glitschka Studios

2A Ⓓ HMK Archive Ⓒ NPR KSTX   2B Ⓓ Fuego3 Ⓒ Weapon Records   2C Ⓓ delit-k-delice Ⓒ urban records   2D Ⓓ MEME ENGINE Ⓒ ANYISM   3A Ⓓ IMAGWHAUS Ⓒ University of Minnesota

3B Ⓓ Carbone Smolan Agency Ⓒ Chicago Symphony Orchestra   3C Ⓓ Whaley Design, Ltd Ⓒ Withrow Ballroom, Katrina Relief Concert   3D Ⓓ Savage Synapses Unltd. Ⓒ Wyclef Jean/Yclef Records

4A Ⓓ Sommese Design Ⓒ Penn State Jazz Club   4B Ⓓ Associated Advertising Agency, Inc. Ⓒ KACY Radio   4C Ⓓ Associated Advertising Agency, Inc. Ⓒ KACY Radio   4D Ⓓ Fox Parlor Ⓒ Wendy Tremont king

5A Ⓓ Blacktop Creative Ⓒ American Jazz Museum   5B Ⓓ Glitschka Studios Ⓒ Brian Carlson Drumming   5C Ⓓ Werner Design Werks Ⓒ VH1   5D Ⓓ Monster Design Company Ⓒ Benicia Performing Arts Foundation

	A	B	C	D
1				
2				
3				
4				
5				

ⓓ = Design Firm   ⓖ = Client

1A ⓓ Werner Design Werks ⓖ Werner Design Werks Inc.   1B ⓓ Gardner Design ⓖ Russell Public Relations   1C ⓓ Henjum Creative ⓖ Language Links   1D ⓓ Banowetz + Company, Inc. ⓖ GLAAD

2A ⓓ FUSZION Collaborative ⓖ CADCA   2B ⓓ Strange Ideas ⓖ bad idea   2C ⓓ HRM ⓖ John E. H. Butler   2D ⓓ Steven O'Connor ⓖ Cyphon Design

3A ⓓ Little Jacket ⓖ Local Girl Gallery   3B ⓓ Owen Design ⓖ Principal   3C ⓓ Jon Flaming Design ⓖ Helen Houp   3D ⓓ Bronson Ma Creative ⓖ Deep Ellum

4A ⓓ Davies Associates ⓖ Cox Paint   4B ⓓ Crackerbox ⓖ Gigi Hair Salon   4C ⓓ Tunglid Advertising Agency ehf. ⓖ Haircastle   4D ⓓ Banowetz + Company, Inc. ⓖ Dean Banowetz

5A ⓓ Gardner Design ⓖ A&M Upholstery   5B ⓓ ComGroup ⓖ Kevin Rowley   5C ⓓ Rule29 ⓖ Rockport Publishers   5D ⓓ Idle Hands Design ⓖ (student project)

LOGO SEARCH

Keywords: **Miscellaneous**

Type: ○ Symbol ○ Typographic ○ Combo ● All

 dataTrust

ROMANO®

DAVIDSON ENTERPRISES

ATLAS
BOOKS

ALLWOOD

DINABEAN

DRUM
DF
FOUNDRY

CLAIM
S
TO FAME

BELISLE
CONSTRUCTION

Bad IDEAS

TCP

SEXICIDE
FLAMMABLE

SEARCH

DUO
COMMUNICATIONS
the power of two

Ⓓ = Design Firm   Ⓒ = Client

1C Ⓓ Axiom Design Group Ⓒ dataTrust 1D Ⓓ Sergio Bianco Ⓒ romano 1956

2A Ⓓ Brainding Ⓒ Davidson Enterprises 2B Ⓓ Eric Baker Design Assoc. Inc. Ⓒ Atlas Books 2C Ⓓ Wallace Church, Inc. Ⓒ Allwood Construction 2D Ⓓ Zipper Design Ⓒ DINABEAN

3A Ⓓ Brian Sooy & Co. Ⓒ Black Swamp Percussion 3B Ⓓ Whaley Design, Ltd Ⓒ Business Incentives 3C Ⓓ Blue Tricycle, Inc. Ⓒ Bursch Brothers, Inc. 3D Ⓓ Ross Hogin Design Ⓒ Ray Belisle

4A Ⓓ Strange Ideas Ⓒ idea bomb 4B Ⓓ Strange Ideas Ⓒ Bad Ideas 4C Ⓓ Dirty Design Ⓒ TC&P 4D Ⓓ Sayles Graphic Design, Inc. Ⓒ Sexicide Band

5A Ⓓ Werner Design Werks Ⓒ Textbooks.com 5B Ⓓ MEME ENGINE Ⓒ ANYISM 5C Ⓓ Bull's-Eye Creative Communication Ⓒ Duo Communications 5D Ⓓ HuebnerPetersen Ⓒ Lori Field, Interior Designer

	A	B	C	D

1

THE WOODS

2

3

m o x i e   ·A LITTLE BLACK DRESS·

4

luckybar   DEUCE creative

5

LOGO SEARCH

Keywords **Food**

Type: ○ Symbol ○ Typographic ○ Combo ● All

LANGUAGE
OF THE LEAF™

Good tea spoken here

RIVERSIDE
COFFEE

wicked café

	A	**B**	**C**	**D**

1

core.

THE MOVEABLE FEAST
School Lunch Service

all stirred up

2

Hill of Beans

3

4

5

CHEESESMITH

sweet dreams bakery

1A 🅓 Element 🅒 Core Financial Services   1B 🅓 Design Nut 🅒 Round House Theatre   1C 🅓 4sight Communications 🅒 Moveable Feast   1D 🅓 MANMADE 🅒 All Stirred Up

2A 🅓 David Kampa 🅒 H.E.B. Foodstores   2B 🅓 Gardner Design 🅒 Material Comforts   2C 🅓 Delikatessen 🅒 Brinkhoffs   2D 🅓 Coleman Creative 🅒 Hill of Beans Coffee House

3A 🅓 Blattner Brunner 🅒 Sister's Place, Inc.   3B 🅓 UNO 🅒 Target Stores   3C 🅓 reduced fat 🅒 Michele Morris   3D 🅓 The Envision Group 🅒 Sweet Peas

4A 🅓 GingerBee Creative 🅒 Farm in the Dell   4B 🅓 Entermotion Design Studio 🅒 In The Sauce Brands Inc.   4C 🅓 HMK Archive 🅒 Anabelle Ardid   4D 🅓 Special Modern Design 🅒 Special Modern Design

5A 🅓 UNO 🅒 Schreiber Foods   5B 🅓 silvercreativegroup 🅒 Tim Smith   5C 🅓 Steve's Portfolio 🅒 Sweet Dreams Bakery   5D 🅓 David Kampa 🅒 H.E.B. Foodstores

A	B	C	D	
				1
				2
				3
				4
				5

Old Dog, New Tricks.

 VUELVE A LA VIDA

wote — women on the edge washington professionals dishing over lunch

Ⓓ = Design Firm   Ⓒ = Client

1A Ⓓ Hayes + Company Ⓒ Liberty Village BIA   1B Ⓓ Actual Size Creative Ⓒ Roadside Ribs   1C Ⓓ Bryan Cooper Design Ⓒ Wiener Works   1D Ⓓ GSD&M Ⓒ Texas BBQ Academy

2A Ⓓ Landor Associates Ⓒ Baked Lays   2B Ⓓ Tribe Design Houston Ⓒ Dart Pizza   2C Ⓓ Nick Glenn Design Ⓒ Zeek's Pizzeria   2D Ⓓ urbanINFLUENCE design studio Ⓒ LaVita é Bella Ristorante

3A Ⓓ ellen bruss design Ⓒ The Oven Pizza e Vino   3B Ⓓ M3 Advertising Design Ⓒ toss Restaurant   3C Ⓓ Farah Design, Inc. Ⓒ San Antonio Wine   3D Ⓓ Actual Size Creative Ⓒ Soirée Catering

4A Ⓓ 4signt Communications Ⓒ Moveable Feast   4B Ⓓ Fauxkoi Ⓒ Lara Miklasevics   4C Ⓓ Wallace Church, Inc. Ⓒ TizNow Restaurant   4D Ⓓ BatesNeimand Ⓒ BatesNeimand

5A Ⓓ Diagram Ⓒ Culinaria Restaurant   5B Ⓓ GSD&M Ⓒ Jackpot Buffet   5C Ⓓ idGO Advertising Ⓒ Meal Works   5D Ⓓ Sandstrom Design Ⓒ Noodlin'

Emory University
Identity Design

Joe Bosack Graphic Design Company, Pipersville, Pennsylvania

Joe Bosack Graphic Design Company is one of handful of design firms that specialize in sports branding. It's an endlessly interesting field, Joe Bosack says, but one of its main pitfalls is that the majority of his office's designs are redesigns of logos with which fans have longstanding and emotional relationships.

"People are passionate about their sports teams. A team's logo directly represents those passions, and when you start to mess with it, especially at the collegiate level, fans can get upset," he says.

That's why the logo Bosack created for the Emory Eagles of Emory University was a refreshing change of pace: No one had any allegiance whatsoever to the athletic department's old logo — essentially a clip art eagle that looked like it had a bad headache.

The project presented unique challenges. Emory University is best known for academics, although some of its athletic teams are national contenders. Its tennis team is a national champion. Trouble is, tennis is not a sport that brings rabid fans out in droves. And the school does not have a football team at all.

In discussions with his client, Bosack discovered that the athletic department wanted a logo that was strong but not overly aggressive or mean-looking, as many college athletic mascot logos are. No exposed, flared talons, he says. The goal was to develop an identity that fit within the overall perception of Emory.

This is a well-respected, elite institution, and the identity we developed reinforces that perception."

He began his work by considering Emory University's logo, a new design that was the outcome of a recent institutional rebranding. The new logo featured a shield shape, and Bosack thought this held promise as an effective connector to athletics.

Another element he found interesting was the letter E. As he explored its shape, he came upon numerous ways to transform the letterform into an eagle or part of an eagle. In the end, the favorite design of the ten Bosack presented was an impassive eagle, its head serving alone as the centerpiece of a shield or as the crossbar on an E.

Almost as important as the logo in sports branding are the colors that are selected, Bosack explains. Emory's school colors are royal blue and a bright gold — not fashionable or "wearable" colors, he felt. Outside of athletic uniforms, in fact, the colors were rarely seen on campus. So Bosack toned the scheme down to a navy blue and a mustard yellow.

The more muted system also helped make accurate reproduction easier to achieve: Many unrelated vendors must be relied on to furnish branded products. "We have to consider what will be practical when the client translates work to the practical world, whether that's through uniforms or decals or whatever," he says.

(Below) Original design

LOGO SEARCH

Keywords **Structures**

Type: ◯ Symbol ◯ Typographic ◯ Combo ⦿ All

	A	B	C	D
1				
2				
3				
4				
5				

ⓓ = Design Firm ⓒ = Client

1C ⓓ Timpano Group ⓒ Healthy Home Reports 1D ⓓ Entermotion Design Studio ⓒ Digital Brand

2A ⓓ Boelts/Stratford Associates ⓒ Renter Rights 2B ⓓ Mirko Ilic Corp ⓒ The Orphan Society of America 2C ⓓ Yellow Fin Studio ⓒ Housing Works Austin 2D ⓓ A3 Design ⓒ Mattamy Homes

3A ⓓ Savage Design Group ⓒ The Joy School 3B ⓓ Paul Black Design ⓒ Centex 3C ⓓ Blattner Brunner ⓒ Beacon House 3D ⓓ Jason Pillon ⓒ Dawn Marie-Tragoutsis

4A ⓓ Fernandez Design ⓒ eTrust 4B ⓓ Carol Gravelle Graphic Design ⓒ Fidelity National Real Estate Solutions 4C ⓓ Sire Advertising ⓒ Harie Insurance Exchange 4D ⓓ Actual Size Creative ⓒ unused

5A ⓓ Dotzero Design ⓒ Office of Sustainable Dev. 5B ⓓ Design One ⓒ Isgrig Mortgage Group 5C ⓓ Brook Group, LTD ⓒ House of Ruth, Maryland 5D ⓓ marc usa ⓒ Indianapolis Neighborhood Housing Partners

	A	B	C	D

1				
2				
3				
4				
5				

	A	B	C	D	

CHACAO

 Colonial Beach BAPTIST CHURCH *A Lighthouse for God*

 ESCAPES TO NEW YORK

1

 3D *Motion*

 GOTHAM BOOKS

2

 O·U·R SAVIOR'S CHURCH

 PORTOLA SPRINGS IRVINE

 UFFIZI GALLERY

 BONJOUR DE PARIS

3

 KIRBYLOFTS

 CASTLE ROCK MASONRY

4

ASYLUM

5

Ⓓ = Design Firm   Ⓒ = Client

	A	B	C	D
1				
2				
3				
4				
5				

LOGO SEARCH

Keywords  **Transportation**

Type: ○ Symbol ○ Typographic ○ Combo ● All

	A	B	C	D	
1					1
2					2
3					3
4					4
5					5

	A	B	C	D
1				
2				
3				
4				
5				

 = Design Firm   © = Client

1A Ⓓ Jon Flaming Design Ⓒ Red Cab Design   1B Ⓓ Fresh Oil Ⓒ AudioStop   1C Ⓓ Felixsockwell.com Ⓒ goodwill   1D Ⓓ Sterling Brands Ⓒ Artwagen

2A Ⓓ judson design associates Ⓒ glasswall Restaurant   2B Ⓓ sheean design Ⓒ Unfiltered Napa   2C Ⓓ Ross Creative + Strategy Ⓒ We Care Transport   2D Ⓓ Sockeye Creative Ⓒ Red Truck Publishing

3A Ⓓ GSD&M Ⓒ Trout Trucking   3B Ⓓ TBF Creative Ⓒ Bak-A-Bush Adventures   3C Ⓓ Reynolds + Associates Ⓒ Indianapolis Police Motorcycle Drill Team   3D Ⓓ Matt Whitley Ⓒ Indy Motor Speedway

4A Ⓓ Brainding Ⓒ Motorcycle   4B Ⓓ R&R Partners Ⓒ Moto Logo   4C Ⓓ R&R Partners Ⓒ Throttle 2   4D Ⓓ Motorcycle Safety Foundation Ⓒ Scooter School

5A Ⓓ David Kampa Ⓒ Texas Bicycle Coalition   5B Ⓓ Greg Walters Design Ⓒ BreakAway Consulting   5C Ⓓ Sandstrom Design Ⓒ adidas   5D Ⓓ Strange Ideas Ⓒ shark racing

	A	B	C	D
1				
2				
3				
4				
5				

index

Log onto www.logolounge.com/book3 for free electronic access to a database of the logos in this book. Search for logos by keywords, client or design firm name, client industry, or type of mark, and get designer credits and contact information along with the logos. For access to nearly 40,000 logos using the same search function, purchase a membership to www.logolounge.com. The collection is always growing: In fact, your membership also allows you to upload an unlimited number of your own logos to be considered by our judges for inclusion in the next LogoLounge book.

directory

(twentystar)
United States
303.596.4134
www.twentystar.com

1 Trick Pony
United States
646.485.8831
www.1trickpony.com

28 LIMITED BRAND
Germany
49.20.939.4238
www.mircommedia.de

2cdesign
United States
214.599.9078
www.2cdesign.com

343 Creative
United States
718.720.7779
www.343creative.com

38one
United Kingdom
44.79.6823.8671
www.38one.com

4sight Communication
United States
323.954.3550
www.get4sight.com

68Design
United States
404.861.5756
www.68design.com

9fps
United States
312.697.1530
www.9fps.net

9MYLES, Inc.
United States
858.344.8619
www.9myles.com

A3 Design
United States
704.568.5351
www.athreedesign.com

Actual Size Creative
United States
412.421.3279
www.thisisactualsize.com

adbass:designs LLC
United States
516.285.0385
www.adbassdesigns.com

Addison Whitney
United States
704.347.5700
www.addisonwhitney.com

AKOFA Creative
United States
404.915.8127
www.akofa.com

Alesce
United States
303.229.8100
www.alesce.com

Ali Cindoruk
United States
212.673.5517
www.alicindoruk.com

Allen Creative
United States
770.972.8862
www.allencreative.com

Alphabet Arm Design
United States
617.451.9990
www.alphabetarmdesign.com

America Online
United States
614.538.4632
www.netscape.com

Ammunition
United Kingdom
44.207.241.2233
www.ammunition.uk

amyHELLER design
United States
203.773.1988
www.amyhellerdesign.com

angryporcupine*design
United States
435.655.0645
www.angryporcupine.com

Anoroc
United States
919.821.1191
www.anorocagency.com

Archrival
United States
402.435.2525
www.archrival.com

Ardoise Design
Canada
514.287.1002
www.ardoise.com

Armeilia Subianto Design
Indonesia
62.21.527.4364
www.asubiantodesign.com

Armstrong International CI
China
86.10.8472.0531
www.AICI.cn

ArtGraphics.ru
Russia
7.095.730.5233
www.artgraphics.ru

ASGARD
Russia
7.812.389.0631
www.asgard-design.com

Associated Advertising Agency, Inc.
United States
316.683.4691
www.associatedadv.com

Atha Design
United States
641.673.2820

Aurora Design
United States
518.346.6228
www.auroradesignonline.com

Axiom Design Group
United States
713.523.5711
www.axiomdg.com

Axiom Design Partners
Western Australia
61.8.9381.6270
www.axiomdp.com.au

B.L.A. Design Company
United States
803.518.4130

b5 Marketing & Kommunikation GmbH
Germany
49.06201.8790731
www.b5-media.de

baba designs
United States
248.360.1251
www.anniewidmyer.com

Bakken Creative Co.
United States
510.540.8260
www.bakkencreativeco.com

Banowetz + Company, Inc.
United States
214.823.7300
www.banowetz.com

Barnstorm Creative
United States
719.630.7200
www.barnstormcreative.biz

Barnstorm Creative Group Inc.
Canada
604.681.3377
www.barnstormcreative.com

batesneimand inc.
United States
202.637.9732
www.batesneimand.com

BCM/D
United States
410.290.5290

Bemporad Baranowski Marketing Group
United States
212.473.4902
www.bbmg.com

Big Bald Guy Design Studio
United States
303.843.9777
www.envision-grp.com

Blacktop Creative
United States
816.221.1585
www.blacktopcreative.com

Blattner Brunner
United States
412.995.9585
www.blattnerbrunner.com

BLOOM LLC
United States
415.451.1866
www.bloommedia.com

Blue Storm Design
New Zealand
64.4.562.8771
www.bluestormdesign.co.nz

Blue Studios, Inc.
United States
410.342.3600
www.bluestudios.com

Blue Tricycle, Inc.
United States
612.729.2372
www.bluetricycle.com

Boelts/Stratford Associates
United States
520.792.1026
www.boeltsstratford.com

Bonilla Design
United States
847.791.3491

Boom Creative
United States
216.291.2411
www.boom-creative.com

Born to Design
United States
317.838.9404
www.born-to-design.com

Brady Design Ltd.
United States
614.299.6661
www.bradydesignltd.com

Brainding
Argentina
www.brainding.com.ar

Brand Bird
United States
404.373.2950
www.brandbird.com

Brand Engine
United States
415.339.4220
www.brandengine.com

Brand Navigation
United States
541.549.4425
www.brandnavigation.com

Brandesign
United States
609.490.9700
www.brandesign.com

Brandia
Portugal
351.213.923000
www.brandia.net

Brandient
Romania
40.21.222.8167
www.brandient.com

BrandSavvy, Inc.
United States
303.471.9991
www.brandsavvyinc.com

Braue; Branding & Corporate Design
Germany
49.471.983820
www.braue.info

Brian Blankenship
United States
817.917.8379
www.brianblankenship.com

Brian Collins Design
United States
417.890.5933
www.williamscollins.com

Brian Sooy & Co.
United States
440.322.5142
www.briansooy.com

Bright Strategic Design
United States
310.305.2565
www.brightdesign.com

Bristol-Myers Squibb Company
United States
609.897.3143
www.bms.com

Bronson Ma Creative
United States
214.457.5615
www.bronsonma.com

Brook Group, LTD
United States
410.465.7805
www.brookgroup.com

Bryan Cooper Design
United States
918.732.3333
www.bryancooperdesign.com
www.cooperillustration.com

Bull's-Eye Creative Communications
United States
404.352.3006
www.bullseyecreative
communications.com

Bunch
Croatia
385.14.920855
www.bunchdesign.com

C. Cady Design
United States
423.843.0456
www.ccadydesign.com

Campbell Fisher Design
United States
602.955.2707
www.thinkcfd.com

CAPSULE
United States
612.341.4525
www.capsule.us

Carbone Smolan Agency
United States
212.807.0011
www.carbonsmolan.com

Carol Gravelle Graphic Design
United States
805.383.2773
www.carolgravelledesign.com

Catch Design Studio
United States
206.322.4323
www.catchstudio.com

Cato Purnell Partners
Australia
61.3.9429.6577
www.catopartners.com

cc design
United States
423.926.3737

CDI Studios
United States
702.876.3316
www.cdistudios.com

Cfx
United States
314.968.1161
www.cfx-inc.com

CH & LER Design
United States
801.966.9171

Chad Carr Design/Westcarr
United States
612.331.4350
www.westcarr.com

Cheri Gearhart, graphic design
United States
708.34634855
www.gearhartdesign.com

Chimera Design
Australia
61.3.9593.6844
www.chimera.com.au

Chris Malven Design
United States
515.450.9023
www.chrismalven.com

christiansen: creative
United States
715.381.8480
www.christiansencreative.com

Church Logo Gallery
United States
760.231.9368
www.churchlogogallery.com

Cisneros Design
United States
505.471.6699
www.cisnerosdesign.com

Clark Studios
United States
949.351.5925
www.clark-studios.com

Coleman Creative
United States
832.797.1682

Colle + McVoy
United States
952.852.7500
www.collemcvoy.com

ComGroup
United States
404.892.4474
www.comgroupmra.com

Communique Group
United States
303.220.5080
www.thecommuniquegroup.com

CONCEPTiCONS
United States
818.259.2725
www.concepticons.com

concussion, llc
United States
817.336.6824
www.concussion.net

Corduroy
United States
214.827.3007
www.corduroydesign.com

Corporate Express
United States
303.664.2000
www.CorporateExpress.com

Cotterteam
United States
410.276.3794
www.nitrobranddesign.com

Crackerbox
United States
617.437.7549
www.crackerbox.us

Creative Kong
United States
512.589.6160
www.creativekong.com

Crescent Lodge
United Kingdom
44.0.20.7613.0613
www.crescentlodge.co.uk

CS Design
United States
320.493.5854

Curtis Sayers Design
United States
617.947.2720
www.csayersdesign.com

Curtis Sharp Design
United States
206.366.7975
www.curtissharpdesign.com

d4 creative group
United States
215.483.4555
www.d4creative.com

dale harris
Australia
41.189.9840
www.daleharris.com

Dan Rood Design
United States
785.842.4870
www.danrooddesign.com

dandy idea
United States
512.627.9103
www.dandyidea.com

Dashwood Design Ltd
New Zealand
64.9307.0901
www.dashwooddesign.com.nz

David Kampa
United States
512.636.3791
www.kampadesign.com

David Maloney Design
United States
612.396.2548
www.david-maloney.com

David Russell Design
United States
206.621.1360
www.davidrusselldesign.com

Davies Associates
United States
310.247.9572
www.daviesla.com

davpunk!
United States
847.345.7865
www.davpunk.com

Day Six Creative
United States
972.548.7337
www.daysixcreative.com

DDB
United States
312.552.6124
www.ddb.com

DDB Dallas
United States
214.259.4200
www.ddbdallas.com

dedstudios
United States
310.850.2161

Deep Design
United States
404.266.7500
www.deepdesign.com

Delikatessen
Germany
49.40.350.8060
www.delikatessen-hamburg.com

delit-k-delice
France
33.1.499.771.984
www.absolutely-design.com

Desgrippes Gobé
United States
212.979.8900
www.dga.com

Design and Image
United States
303.292.3455
www.designandimage.com

Design MG/DMG
Panama
507.214.1781.1700

Design Nut
United States
301.942.2360
www.designnut.com

Design One
United States
828.254.7898
www.d1inc.com

designlab, inc
United States
314.962.7702
www.designlabinc.com

Designsensory
United States
865.690.2249
www.designsensory.com

design-studio Muhina
Russia
7.3412.76.3315
www.muhina.com

Deuce Creative
United States
713.863.8633
www.deucecreative.com

Diagram
Poland
48.61.664.8081
www.diagram.pl

Dialekt Design
Canada
450.226.1440
www.dialektdesign.com

DIRECT DESIGN
Visual Branding
Russia
7.095.916.01.23
www.directdesign.ru

Dirty Design
United Kingdom
44.0.117.927.3344
www.dirtydesign.co.uk

Ditto!
United States
914.478.3641
www.dittodoesit.com

dmayne design
United States
417.823.8058
www.dmaynedesign.com

Doink, Inc.
United States
305.529.0121
www.doinkdesign.com

Dotfive
United States
415.354.1076
www.dotfive.com

Dotzero Design
United States
503.892.9262
www.DotzeroDesign.com

Doug Beatty
Canada
416.826.3684
www.taxizone.com

Dr. Alderete
Mexico
52.55.1998.4688
www.jorgealderete.com

Dreamedia Studios
United States
501.954.9711
www.dreamediastudios.com

Duffy & Partners
United States
612.548.2333
www.duffy.com

Eben Design
United States
206.523.9010
www.ebendesign.com

Edward Allen
United States
512.443.2102

eindruck design
United States
406.829.1581
www.eindruckdesign.com

Eisenberg and Associates
United States
214.528.5990
www.eisenberg-inc.com

Elaine Park
United States
312.384.1906
www.commongroundmktg.com

Element
United States
614.447.0906
www.elementville.com

Elephant in the Room
United States
336.624.9844
www.elephantintheroom.biz

Eleven Feet Media
United States
650.278.2451
www.elevenfeetmedia.com

elf design
United States
650.358.9973
www.elf-design.com

ellen bruss design
United States
303.830.8323
www.ebd.com

emblem
Venezuela
58.212.243.2969
www.mblm.com

Emphasize LLC
United States
718.932.7810
www.mariavilla.com

Entermotion Design Studio
United States
316.264.2277
www.entermotion.com

Enterprise
South Africa
27.11.319.8000
www.enterpriseig.co.zg

Eric Baker Design Assoc., Inc.
United States
212.598.9111
www.ericbakerdesign.com

Exti Dzyn
United States
818.679.9116
www.extidzyn.com

Eyebeam Creative LLC
United States
202.518.5888
www.eyebeamcreative.com

Eyescape
United Kingdom
44.0.20.8521.0342
www.eyescape.co.uk

fallindesign studio
Russia
7.812.461.1985
www.faldin.ru

Farah Design, Inc.
United States
786.267.2954
www.farahdesign.com &
www.visiom.com

Farm Design
United States
310.828.1624
www.farmdesign.net

Fauxkoi
United States
612.251.4277
www.fauxkoi.com

Felixsockwell.com
United States
917.657.8880
www.felixsockwell.com

Fernandez Design
United States
512.619.4020
www.fernandezdesign.com

Fifth Letter
United States
336.723.5655
www.fifth-letter.com

FigDesign
United States
972.259.5900
www.figdesign.com

FiveStone
United States
678.730.0686
www.fivestone.com

Flaxenfield, Inc.
United States
336.218.0530
www.flaxenfield.com

Floor 84 Studio
United States
818.754.1231
www.floor84studio.com

Formikula
Germany
49.0.89.48.00.45.64
www.marc-herold.com

Fox Parlor
United States
415.821.7100
www.foxparlor.com

Franke+Fiorella
United States
612.338.1700
www.frankefiorella.com

Fredrik Lewander
Sweden
46.73.955.9968
www.fredriklewander.se

Fresh Oil
United States
401.709.4656
www.freshoil.com

Freshwater Design
United States
678.910.6381
www.freshwaterdesign.net

Fuego3
United States
817.937.1605
www.fuego3.com

Funk/Levis & Associates, Inc.
United States
541.485.1932
www.funklevis.com

FUSZION Collaborative
United States
703.548.8080
www.fuszion.com

FutureBrand
United States
212.931.6300
www.futurebrand.com

FutureBrand Melbourne
Australia
61.3.9604.2777
www.futurebrand.com

FutureBrand Buenos Aires
Argentina
54.11.4777.2277
www.futurebrand.com

Fuze
United States
775.626.4577
www.ifuze.com

FWIS
United States
503.230.1741
www.fwis.com

Gabi Toth
Romania
4.072.253.3715
www.toth.ro

Gabriel Kalach *
V I S U A L communications
United States
305.532.2336

Gabriela Gasparini Design
United States
718.417.1064
www.gabrielagasparini.com

Gardner Design
United States
316.691.8808
www.gardnerdesign.com

Garfinkel Design
United States
706.369.6831
www.garfinkeldesign.com

Gee + Chung Design
United States
415.543.1192
www.geechungdesign.com

Gee Creative
United States
843.853.3086
www.geecreative.com

GetElevatedDesign.com
United States
www.ejhartley.com

ginger griffin marketing and design
United States
704.896.2479
www.wehaveideas.com

GingerBee Creative
United States
406.443.3032
www.gingerbee.com

Glitschka Studios
United States
971.223.6143
www.vonglitschka.com

Goldforest
United States
305.573.7370
www.goldforest.com

GRAF d'SIGN creative boutique
Russia
7.916.686.2812
www.gdscb.com

GrafiQa Graphic Design
United States
607.433.8837
www.grafiqa.com

Grapefruit
Romania
40.232.233.066

Greg Walters Design
United States
206.362.1310

greteman group
United States
316.263.1004
www.gretemangroup.com

Gridwerk
United States
215.872.6266
www.gridwerk.net

GSCS
United Arab Emirates
971.4391.0873
www.greggsedgwick.com

GSD&M
United States
512.242.4602
www.gsdm.com

Haley Johnson Design
United States
612.722.8050
haley@hja.com

Hallmark Cards Inc.
United States
816.545.6753
www.hallmark.com

Hammerpress
United States
816.421.1929
www.hammerpress.net

Hanna & Associates
United States
208.661.9455
www.cdaoriginals.com

HardBall Sports
United States
904.998.8778
www.hardballcreative.com

Harkey Design
United States
404.609.9090
www.harkeydesign.com

Harwood Kirsten Leigh McCoy
South Africa
27.83.441.0174
www.hklm.co.za

Hat-trick Design Consultants
United Kingdom
44.0.20.7403.7875
www.hat-trickdesign.co.uk

Hausch Design Agency LLC
United States
414.628.3976
www.hauschdesign.com

Hayes + Company
Canada
416.536.5438
www.hayesandcompany.com

Henjum Creative
United States
920.866.3738

Hill Design Studios
United States
503.507.1228
www.hilldesignstudios.com

Hinge
United States
703.391.8870
www.pivotalbrands.com

Hipflix.com/The 5659 Design Co.
United States
773.685.7019
www.hipflix.com

Hirshorn Zuckerman Design Group
United States
301.294.6302

HMK Archive
United States
210.473.1961
www.sharkthang.com

Honey Design
Canada
519.679.0786
www.honey.on.ca

Hope Advertising
Australia
61.3.9529.7799
www.hope.com.au

Hornall Anderson
United States
206.826.2329
www.hadw.com

Howerton + White Interactive
United States
316.262.6644
www.howertonwhite.com

Howling Good Designs
United States
631.427.4769
www.howlinggooddesigns.com

Hoyne Design
Australia
61.39.537.1822
www.hoyne.com.au

HRM
United States
985.879.2443
www.hrmcreative.com

Hubbell Design Works
United States
714.227.3457
www.hubbelldesignworks.com

HuebnerPetersen
United States
970.663.9344

humanot
United States
716.604.4026
www.humanot.com

Hutchinson Associates, Inc.
United States
312.455.9191
www.hutchinson.com

i3design
United States
610.828.6442
www.i3design.us

i4 Solutions
United States
801.294.6400
www.i4.net

Idea Girl Design
United States
310.623.2288
www.ideagirldesign.com

idGO Advertising
United States
401.368.1049

Idle Hands Design
United States
917.690.2383
www.idlehandsnyc.com

Ikola designs
United States
763.533.3440

IMA Design, Corp.
Russia
7.095.262.5985
www.lmadesign.ru

IMAGEHAUS
United States
612.377.8700
www.imagehaus.net

Imaginaria
United States
214.257.8704
www.imaginariacreative.com

INNFUSION Studios
United States
800.996.7616
www.innfusionstudios.com

Insight Design
United States
316.262.0085

Insomniac Creative Studio
United States
www.insomniaccs.com

Integer Group - Midwest
United States
515.288.7910
www.interger.com

Interrobang Design Collaborative, Inc.
United States
802.434.5970
www.interrobangdesign.com

Intersection Creative
United States
602.622.8757
www.intersectioncreative.com

Iperdesign, Inc.
United States
917.412.9045
www.iperdesign.com

ivan2design
United States
206.364.8996
www.ivan2.com

j6Studios
www.j6studios.com

Jason Kirshenblatt/ The O Group
United States
212.398.0100
www.ogroup.net

Jason Pillon
United States
925.243.1936

JC Thomas Marketing/ Advertising
United States
704.377.9660
www.thoughtville.com

Jeff Pollard Design
United States
503.246.7251
www.jpd-logos.com

Jejak, Rumah Iklan dan Disain
Indonesia
62.21.722.3306
www.jejak.net

Jenny Kolcun Freelance Design
United States
415.331.7202

joe miller's company
United States
408.988.2924

Joi Design
New Zealand
649.377.6684
www.joi.co.nz

Jon Flaming Design
United States
972.235.4880
www.jonflaming.com

Jonathan Rice & Company
United States
817.886.6640
www.jriceco.com

josh higgins design
United States
619.379.2090
www.joshhiggins.com

joven orozco design
United States
949.723.1898
www.jovenville.com

jsDesignCo.
United States
614.353.6412

judson design associates
United States
713.520.1096
www.judsondesign.com

juls design inc
United States
515.963.8309
www.julsdesign.com

Justin Johnson
United States
918.519.1605
www.morebranding.com

Justin Lockwood Design
United States
206.529.7585
www.justinlockwooddesign.com

Kahn Design
United States
760.944.5574
www.kahn-design.com

Kaimere
United Arab Emirates
971.4391.8083
www.tmh.ae

Kendall Creative Shop, Inc.
United States
214.827.6680
www.kendallcreative.com

Kendall Ross
United States
206.262.0540
www.kendallross.com

Kern Design Group
United States
203.329.7070
www.kerndesigngroup.com

Kevin France Design, Inc.
United States
336.765.6213

Keyword Design
United States
219.923.5279
www.keyworddesign.com

Kinesis, Inc.
United States
541.482.3600
www.kinesisinc.com

Kineto
Indonesia
62.21.831.7106
www.kineto.biz

Kitemath
United States
773.252.9908
www.kitemath.com

KOESTER design
United States
469.621.6566
www.koesterdesign.com

KONG Design Group
United States
714.478.9657
www.kongdesigngroup.com

KURT FOR HIRE
United States
917.771.4142
www.kurtforhire.com

KW43 BRANDDESIGN
Germany
49.200.557.7830
www.kw43.gr

Kym Abrams Design
United States
312.654.1005
www.kad.com

label brand
United States
831.421.0518
www.labelbrand.com

Lance Reed/ tmh the Media House
United Arab Emirates
971.4391.8083
www.tmh.ae

LandDesign
United States
703.549.7784
www.landdesign.com

Landkamer Partners, Inc.
United States
415.522.2480
www.landkamerpartners.com

Landor Associates
United States
212.614.5261
www.landor.com

Lars Lawson
United States
317.921.0948
www.timberdesignco.com

Lauchpad Creative
United States
405.514.5158
www.launchpad321.com

Leeann Leftwich Zajas Graphic Design
United States
603.702.1044
www.11zdesign.com

Lenox Graphics
United States
401.862.7224
www.lenoxgraphics.com

Les Kerr Creative
United States
972.236.3599
www.leskerr.net

Lesniewicz Associates
United States
419.243.7131
www.designtoinfluence.com

Letter 7
United States
212.595.7445
www.ltr7.com

Lienhart Design
United States
312.738.2200
www.lienhartdesign.com

Lippincott Mercer
United States
212.521.0000
www.lippincottmercer.com

Lisa Speer
United States
917.533.6397
www.lisaspeer.com

Lisa Starace
United States
619.757.6308
www.designactionism.com

Liska + Associates Communication Design
United States
312.644.4400
www.liska.com

Little Jacket
United States
216.373.6979
www.little-jacket.com

Living Creative Design
United States
510.304.0450
www.livingcreative.com

Lizette Gecel
United States
804.359.1711

logobyte design studio
Turkey
90.535.666.6292
www.logobyte.com

LogoDesignSource.com
United States
954.428.8871
www.logodesignsource.com

Lulu Strategy
United States
614.221.3403
www.lulustrategy.com

Lunar Cow
United States
800.594.9620
www.lunarcow.com

Lunar Design
United States
415.252.4388
www.lunar.com

M3 Advertising Design
United States
702.796.6323
www.m3ad.com

Macnab Design Visual Communication
United States
508.286.8558
www.macnabdesign.com

Mad Dog Graphx
United States
907.276.5062
www.thedogpack.com

MANMADE
United States
415.865.9996
www.manmade.com

MannPower Design
United States
973.983.0626
www.mannpowerdesign.com

marc usa
United States
317.632.6501
www.marcusa.com

Maremar Graphic Design
Puerto Rico
787.731.8795
www.maremar.com

Mariqua Design
United States
650.242.4645
www.mariqua.com

markatos
United States
415.235.9203
www.markatos.com

Mary Hutchison Design LLC
United States
206.407.3460
www.maryhutchisondesign.com

Matt Everson Design
United States
608.628.3095
www.matteverson.com

Matt Whitley/Outdoor Cap
United States
479.464.5203
www.outdoorcap.com

mattisimo
United States
415.786.2769
www.mattisimo.com

Mattson Creative
United States
949.388.1772
www.mattsoncreative.com

maximo, inc.
United States
619.269.0063
www.maximoinc.com

Maycreate
United States
423.634.0123
www.maycreate.com

McAndrew Kaps
United States
480.580.5113
www.macandrewkaps.com

mccoycreative
United States
360.920.5260
www.mccoycreative.com

McGuire Design
United States
210.884.4609
www.mcguiredesign.com

McMillian Design
United States
718.636.2097
www.mcmilliandesign.com

MEME ENGINE
United States
212.203.5787
www.memeengine.com

Methodologie
United States
206.623.1044
www.methodologie.com

Metroparks of the Toledo Area
United States
419.407.9735
www.metroparkstoledo.com

Mez Design
United States
715.331.4523
www.mezdesign.com

Miaso Design
United States
773.575.3776
www.miasodesign.com

Michael Courtney Design, Inc.
United States
206.329.8488
www.michaelcourtneydesign.com

Michael Osborne Design
United States
415.255.0125
www.modsf.com

Miles Design
United States
317.915.8693
www.milesdesign.com

Mindgruve
United States
619.757.1325
www.mindgruve.com

Mindspace
United States
480.221.5817
www.mindspaceonline.com

Mindspike Design, LLC
United States
414.765.2344
www.mindspikedesign.com

MINE
United States
415.647.6463
www.minesf.com

Mires/Ball
United States
619.234.6631
www.miresball.com

Miriello Grafico, Inc.
United States
619.234.1124
www.miriellografico.com

Mirko Ilic Corp
United States
212.481.9737
www.mirkoilic.com

Misenheimer Creative, Inc.
United States
770.667.9355
www.misenheimer.com

mixdesign
United States
219.322.7190
www.mixedupworld.com

mk12
United States
816.931.2425
www.mk12.com

Mode Design Studio
United States
214.827.4700
www.modedesignstudio.com

Modern Dog Design Co.
United States
206.789.7667
www.moderndog.com

Mohouse Design Co.
United States
214.321.3193
www.mohousedesign.com

monster design
United States
425.828.7853
www.monsterinvasion.com

Monster Design Company
United States
707.208.5481
www.monsterdesignco.com

Moonsire Design
United States
843.667.3407

Morgan/Mohon
United States
830.990.2888
www.morganmohon.com

morrow mckenzie design
United States
503.222.0331
www.morrowmckenzie.com

Morse and Company Advertising Communication
United States
219.879.1223
www.morseandcompany.com

Moscato Design
United States
630.493.0518

Motorcycle Safety Foundation
United States
949.727.3227
www.msf-usa.org

Motterdesign
Austria
43.5572.3847.0777
www.motter.at

Napoleon design
Brazil
55.11.9935.0300
www.napoleondesign.net

Naughtyfish
Australia
61.2.9327.7942
www.naughtyfish.com

NeoGine Communication Design Ltd.
New Zealand
64.4.385.1792
www.neogine.co.nz

Miles Newlyn/x & y Ltd.
United Kingdom
44.20.7551.4520
contact@newlyn.com

nicelogo
United States
949.677.7324
www.nicelogo.com

Nick Glenn Design
United States
281.814.7976
www.nickglennalesign.com

Nita B. Creative
United States
651.644.2889
www.nitabcreative.com

Noble and Associates
United States
417.875.5000
www.noble.net

northfound
United States
215.232.6420
www.northfound.com

Novasoul
United States
818.753.4175
www.novasoul.com

Tom Nynas/R&D Thinktank
United States
214.515.9515
www.randdthinktank.com

Ó!
Iceland
354.562.3300
www.oid.is

o2 ideas
United States
205.949.9494
www.o2ideas.com

oakley design studios
United States
503.241.3705
www.oakleydesign.com

Octane
United States
775.323.7887
www.octanestudios.com

octane inc.
United States
828.693.6699
www.hi-testdesign.com

Octavo Designs
United States
301.695.8885
www.8vodesigns.com

ODM oficina de diseno y marketing
Spain
34.956.265.326
www.odmoficina.com

Off-Leash Studios
United States
617.821.5158
www.offleashstudios.com

Olson + Company
United States
612.215.9800
www.oco.com

OmniStudio Inc.
United States
202.464.3050
www.omnistudio.com

Onoma, LLC
United States
212.253.6570
www.onomadesign.com

Open
United States
212.645.5633
www.notclosed.com

Orange Creative
New Zealand
64.9.273.3688
www.orangecreative.co.nz

Owen Design
United States
515.244.1515
www.chadowendesign.com

Oxide Design Co.
United States
402.344.0168
www.oxidedesign.com

Parachute Design
United States
612.359.4387
www.parachutedesign.com

Paragon Design International
United States
312.832.1030
www.paragondesign
international.com

pat sinclair design
United States
610.896.8616
www.patsinclairdesign.com

Paul Black Design
United States
214.537.9780
www.paulblackdesign.com

Peak Seven Advertising
United States
954.574.0810
www.peakseven.com

Pennebaker
United States
713.963.8607
www.pennebaker.com

Perfect Circle Media Group
United States
972.788.0678
www.perfect360.com

Peters Design
United States
720.348.1053
www.karlpeters.com

Peterson & Company
United States
214.954.0522
www.peterson.com

Phillips Design
United States
813.253.2523
www.portfolios.com/
phillipsdesign

Pix Design, Inc.
United States
212.563.5701
www.pixdesign.com

Pixel Basement
United States
561.376.1899
www.pixelbasement.com

Pixelspace
United States
828.994.2212
www.pixelspace.com

Pixelube
United States
206.216.0278
www.pixelube.com

Playoff Corporation
United States
817.983.0142

pleitezgallo :: design haus
United States
951.961.1524
www.pleitezgallo.com

Polemic Design
United States
201.978.5677
www.polemicdesign.com

Polkadot
Australia
61.1.300.139.398
www.polkadot.com.au

PosterV.Design Studio
Denmark
45.45.85.3575
www.pocs-posters.hv

PowerGroove Creative
United States
720.529.0143

Praxis Studios
United States
919.838.1138
www.praxisstudios.com

Project center
United States
770.979.7684
www.balkecreative.com

Propeller Design
United Arab Emirates
971.4391.4849
www.propeller.ae

proteus
United States
617.263.2211
www.proteusdesign.com

Q
Germany
49.611.181310
www.q-home.de

Quest Fore
United States
412.381.6670
www.questfore.com

R&D Thinktank
United States
214.515.9851
www.randdthinktank.com

R&R Partners
United States
702.318.4360
www.rrpartners.com

rajasandhu.com
Canada
647.668.2547
www.rajasandhu.com

Ramp
United States
213.617.1445
www.rampcreative.com

Red Circle Agency
United States
612.372.4612
www.redcircleagency.com

reduced fat
United States
518.533.9621
www.reduced-fat.com

rehab* communication graphics
United States
206.794.4209
www.rehabgraphics.com

REINES DESIGN INC.
United States
305.373.3181
www.reinesdesign.com

retropup
United States
973.723.5420
www.retropup.com

Reynolds + Associates
United States
310.698.9330
www.372interactive.com

Richards Brock Miller Mitchell & Associates /RBMM
United States
214.987.6500
www.rbmm.com

Rick Johnson & Company
United States
505.266.1100
www.rjc.com

Rickabaugh Graphics
United States
614.337.2229
www.rickbaughgraphics.com

RIGGS
United States
803.799.5972
www.riggspeak.com

ROAD design inc.
United States
949.494.8020
www.roaddzn.com

ROBOT
United States
210.476.8801
www.robotcreative.com

Robot Agency Studios
United States
832.859.0650
www.robotagency.com

Roger Christian & Co.
United States
210.829.1953
www.warmsprings.org

Rome & Gold Creative
United States
505.897.0870
www.rgcreative.com

Ross Creative + Strategy
United States
309.637.7677
www.rosscps.com

Ross Hogin Design
United States
206.443.3930
www.hogin.com

Rotor Design
United States
763.706.3906
www.rotordesign.net

Rule29
United States
630.262.1009
www.rule29.com

Ryan Cooper
United States
303.917.9911

S Design, Inc.
United States
405.608.0556
www.sdesigninc.com

S4LE.com
Canada
905.467.7139
www.s4le.com

Sabet Branding
United States
949.705.9960
www.sabet.com

Sabingrafik, Inc.
United States
760.431.0439
www.tracy.sabin.com

Sakkal Design
United States
425.483.8830
www.sakkal.com

Sam's Garage
United States
720.320.7220
www.samsgarageonline.com

Sandstrom Design
United States
503.248.9466
www.sandstromdesign.com

sarah watson design
United States
206.545.8682
www.sarahwatsondesign.com

Savage Design Group
United States
713.522.1555
www.savagedesign.com

Savage Synapses Unltd.
United States
443.756.4674
www.flotsandjets.com

Sayles Graphic Design, Inc.
United States
515.279.2922
www.saylesdesign.com

Schuster Design Group
United States
214.632.3328

Scott Oeschger Design
United States
610.497.1101
www.scottoeschger.com

SD Graphic Design
United States
617.523.5144
www.delaneygroup.com

Seed Studios
United States
817.431.1405
www.seedstudios.com

Sergio Bianco
Italy
39.185.77.2289
www.sergiobianco.it

Sharp Communications, Inc.
United States
212.892.0002
www.sharpthink.com

sharp pixel
United States
206.226.1030
www.sharppixel.com

Shawn Hazen Graphic Design
United States
510.594.9271
www.shawnhazen.com

sheean design
United States
707.224.5206
www.sheeandesign.com

Shelley Design + Marketing
United States
410.523.2796
www.shelleyllc.com

Shift design
Portugal
351.21.410.5912
www.shiftdesign.pt

Sibley/ Peteet Design
United States
512.473.2333
www.spdaustin.com

silvercreativegroup
United States
203.855.7705
www.silvercreativegroup.com

Simon & Goetz Design
Germany
49.69.96.88.55.0
www.simongoetz.de

Sire Advertising
United States
570.743.3900
www.sireadvertising.com

SKOOTA
United States
919.824.6487
www.skoota.com

Sockeye Creative
United States
503.226.3843
www.sockeyecreative.com

Soho Joe
United States
612.588.8740
www.sohojoe.com

Solo Multimedia, Inc.
United States
785.841.5500
www.solomultimedia.com

Sommese Design
United States
814.353.1951

soupgraphix
United States
619.749.SOUP
www.soupgraphix.com

Special Modern Design
United States
323.258.1212
www.specialmoderndesign.com

Squires & Company
United States
214.939.9194
www.squirescompany.com

Stacy Bormett Design, LLC
United States
651.748.0872

Stand Advertising
United States
716.210.1065
www.standadvertising.com

Starlight Studio
United States
718.302.5600

Stephan and Herr
United States
717.426.2939
www.stephanherr.com

Sterling Brands
United States
212.329.4600
www.sterlingbrands.com

Steven O'Connor
United States
323.779.5600

Steve's Portfolio
United States
215.840.0880
www.stevesportfolio.net

Stiles + co
United States
503.806.4670
www.stilesandco.com

Stoltze Design
United States
617.350.7109
www.stoltze.com

Straka Dusan/Straka Design
Germany
49.179.126.8229
www.hofd.net

Strange Ideas
United States
316.259.4374

Strategic America
United States
515.453.2000
www.strategicamerica.com

Strategy Studio
United States
212.966.7800
www.strategy-studio.com

strategyone
United States
630.790.9050
www.strategyone.com

stressdesign
United States
315.422.3231
www.stressdesign.com

Studio Arts and Letters
United States
303.298.9911
www.studioartsandletters.com

Studio D
United States
212.563.5600
www.studiodny.com

Studio GT&P
Italy
39.074.232.0372
www.tobanelli.it

Studio Simon
United States
502.479.8447
www.studiosimon.net

Studio Stubborn Sideburn
United States
206.709.8970
www.stubbornsideburn.com

STUN Design and Advertising
United States
225.381.7266
www.stundesign.net

Stuph Clothing
United States
800.242.9166
www.uthstuph.com

Suburban Utopia
United States
706.425.8836
www.suburbanutopia.com

SUMO
United Kingdom
0191.261.9894
www.sumodesign.co.uk

Sutter Design
United States
301.459.5445
www.sutterdesign.com

switchfoot creative
United States
760.720.4255
www.switchfootcreative.com

Synergy Graphix
United States
212.968.7568
www.synergygraphix.com

Tactical Magic
United States
901.722.3001
www.tacticalmagic.com

Tactix Creative
United States
480.225.1480
www.tactixcreative.com

Tallgrass Studios
United States
785.887.6049
www.tallgrassstudios.com

tanagram partners
United States
312.876.3668
www.tanagram.com

TBF Creative
United States
602.722.7995
www.tbfcreative.com

Tchopshop Media
United States
504.895.0000
www.tchopshop.com

tesser inc.
United States
415.541.9999
www.tesser.com

the atmosfear
United States
702.355.8896
www.theatmosfear.com

The Clockwork Group
United States
210.798.1000
www.theclockworkgroup.com

The Collaboration
United States
913.271.3603
www.the-collaboration.com

The Design Poole
United States
206.301.9282
www.thedesignpoole.com

The Envision Group
United States
303.843.9777
www.envision-grp.com

The Flores Shop
United States
804.304.6731
www.thefloresshop.com

The Gate Worldwide
United States
212.508.3400
www.thegateworldwide.com

**The Joe Bosack Graphic
Design Co.**
United States
215.766.1461
www.joebosack.com

The Logo Factory Inc.
Canada
905.564.6747
www.thelogofactory.com

The Meyocks Group
United States
515.225.1200
www.outofthebox.com

The Oesterle
Germany
00.49.89.130.178.74
www.the-oesterle.com

The Pink Pear Design Company
United States
816.519.7327
www.pinkpear.com

The Robin Shepherd Group
United States
904.359.0981
www.trsg.net

The zen kitchen
United States
401.787.5178
www.daniordin.net

thehappycorp global
United States
646.613.1220
www.thehappycorp.com

Thielen Designs
United States
505.396.3900
www.ThielenDesigns.com

Think Tank Creative
United States
337.989.4018

Thomas Manss & Company
United Kingdom
44.20.7251.7777
www.manss.com

thomas-vasquez.com
United States
718.422.1948

Tiffany Design
United States
714.467.8428

Tim Frame Design
United States
937.766.3749
www.timframe.com

Times Infinity
United States
713.224.6200
www.times-infinity.com

Timpano Group
United States
608.251.0808
www.timpanogroup.com

Todd M. LeMieux
United States
413.747.9321
www.toddlemieux.com

Tom Fowler, Inc.
United States
203.845.0700
www.tomfowlerinc.com

Traci Jones design
United States
303.447.8202
www.commarts-boulder.com

Tribe Design
United States
713.523.5119
www.tribedesign.com

Tungld Advertising Agency
Iceland
354.533.2323
www.tungl.is

Turner Duckworth
United States / United Kingdom
415.675.7777
44.0.20.8994.7190
www.TurnerDuckworth.com

Turney Creative
United States
858.349.6370
www.turneycreative.com

Type G
United States
858.792.7333
www.typegdesign.com

Typonic
United Kingdom
44.13.7655.4823
www.typonic.com

Uhlein Design
United States
215.206.2733
www.uhleindesign.com

UlrichPinciotti Design Group
United States
419.255.4515
www.updesigngroup.com

UltraVirgo Creative
United States
646.638.0813
www.ultravirgo.com

Unibrand Belgrade
Turkmenistan
993.81.11.3285.257
www.unibrand360.com

Univisual
Italy
39.02.668.4268
www.univisual.it

UNO
United States
612.874.1920
www.unoonline.com

**urbanINFLUENCE
design studio**
United States
206.219.3599
www.urbaninfluence.com

V V N Design
United States
706.903.2410
www.vvndesign.com

Velocity Design Works
Canada
204.475.0514
www.velocitydesignworks.com

Vigor Graphic Design, LLC.
United States
717.234.4846
www.vigorgraphics.net

Vincent Burkhead Studio
United States
619.787.9384
www.VincentBurkhead.com

Visual Coolness
United States
520.722.6364
www.visualcoolness.com

Visual Inventor Ltd. Co.
United States
405.842.6768
www.VisualInventor.com

Visual Moxie
United States
805.277.4741
www.visualmoxie.com

VMA
United States
937.233.7500
www.vmai.com

Wallace Church, Inc.
United States
212.755.2903
www.wallacechurch.com

Walsh Associates
United States
918.743.9600
www.walshassoc.com

Wells Fargo Financial
United States
515.557.7825

Werner Design Werks
United States
612.338.2550
www.wdw.com

Weylon Smith
United States
615.306.1485

Whaley Design, Ltd
United States
651.645.3463
www.whaleydesign.com

Whence: the studio
United States
504.338.2994
www.michaelnixdesign.com

Whitney Edwards LLC
United States
410.822.8335
www.wedesign.com

Wholesale Distributors
United States
206.290.7017
www.wd-usa.com

**Who's the Min/
Creative Solutions**
United States
973.219.2335
www.whosthemin.com

Wilkinson Media, Inc.
United States
609.818.0363
www.wilkinsonmedia.net

Willoughby Design Group
United States
816.561.4189
www.willoughbydesign.com

Wolken communica
United States
206.545.1696
www.wolkencommunica.com

Wolff Olins
United Kingdom
44.0.20.7713.7733
www.wolff-olins.com

Wray Ward Laseter
United States
704.332.9071
www.wwlcreative.com

www.iseedots.com
United States
619.955.8178
www.iseedots.com

Yellobee Studio
United States
404.249.6407
www.yellobee.com

Yellow Fin Studio
United States
512.472.3227
www.yellowfinstudio.com

**Yellow Pencil
Brand Sharpening**
New Zealand
64.365.0080
www.yellowpencil.co.nz

ykcreative, LLC
United States
832.752.6402
www.ykcreative.com

Zapata Design
United States
281.785.0242
www.zapatadesign.com

ZEBRA Design Branding
Russia
7.8482.485684

**Zed + Zed + Eye
Creative Communications**
United States
352.572.3474
www.zedzedeye.com

zengigi design
United States
301.562.9406
www.zengigi.com

Zipper Design
United States
206.818.9101
www.zipperd.com

Zombie Design
United States
801.299.1567
www.designzombie.com

ZONA Design
United States
212.244.2900
www.zonadesign.com

Zwölf Sonnen Design
Germany
49.06.114.504.942
www.zwoelfsonnen.de

about the authors

Bill Gardner is president of Gardner Design and has produced work for Learjet, Thermos, Nissan, Pepsi, Pizza Hut, Kroger, Hallmark, Cargill Corporation, and the 2004 Athens Olympics. His work has been featured in *Communication Arts*, *Print*, *Graphis*, *New York Art Directors Annual*, *Step Inside Design*, Mead Top 60, the Museum of Modern Art, and many other national and international design exhibitions. He lives in Wichita, Kansas.

Cathy Fishel is a freelance writer and editor who specializes in graphic design. She is the author of many books on the subject; contributes to many magazines, including *PRINT* and *Communication Arts*; and is editor of LogoLounge.com.